A Place to Call Home

The Amazing Success Story
of Modern Orphanages

A Place to Call Home

MARTHA RANDOLPH CARR

 **Prometheus Books**

59 John Glenn Drive
Amherst, New York 14228–2119

Published 2007 by Prometheus Books

Inquiries should be addressed to
Prometheus Books
59 John Glenn Drive
Amherst, New York 14228–2119
VOICE: 716–691–0133, ext. 210
FAX: 716–691–0137
WWW.PROMETHEUSBOOKS.COM

11 10 09 08 07   5 4 3 2 1

Library of Congress Cataloging-in-Publication Data

Carr, Martha Randolph, 1959–
    A place to call home : the amazing success story of modern orphanages / by Martha Randolph Carr.
        p. cm.
    Includes index.
    ISBN 978–1–59102–510–8
    1. Orphanages—United States—History. 2. Orphans—United States—History.
3. Orphans—United States—Interviews. I. Title.

HV983.C37 2007
362.73'2—dc22

2007022517

Printed in the United States of America on acid-free paper

Dedicated in loving memory to my late father,
Rev. Dabney Jefferson Carr III,
to my mother, Leontine, and family,
to my "sisters," Maria, Diane, and Susie,
and to my wonderful son, Louie, who is my inspiration
for his courage, love, and humor.

A very special thank you to:
Maria Wingfield Butler
and Barbara Pedrotty
Heberd Webb
Ed Shipman for his support and words of wisdom
The Happy Hill Farm Academy
Southwest Airlines
Zuki McLaughlan
Girard College
Tod Balsbaugh
The Virginia Home for Boys & Girls
David Tribble and Mr. Mac
Bethesda Home for Boys
Mark Schmeltzer and Brother Brian Maloney
Mercy Home for Boys and Girls
Rev. Sally Perry, Rev. Dwight and Thelma Smith
Bishop Peter Lee
Ron Goldfarb and Lori Ames
Steven L. Mitchell
Roger Canaff
Vera Duke
Juanita Puffenbarger
and Bob Danzig

HOUSE ACROSS THE RIVER
By Maria Wingfield Butler

The house across the silver stretch,
the one the sun sets on in July—
who lives there?
Who sits on the porch
in the summer heat—
stares out its dormers
in February ice storms?

A vigorous row would take me there,
sixty miles by car.

A penny in my outstretched hand
in line with my eye, would blot the house
from view like the morning's long smear
of mist.

I never consider who lives there
unless I'm sitting in this meditation
spot using the river to make
me some connection
between matter and the unknown.

Who lives there?
I pretend to know.

A family with several children
who sing at night,
net crabs on the full moon,
whose children run thru the rooms
in bare feet laughing when the cousins come.

An old man rewriting history
with hasty pen strokes
that make a noise
creating a past.—
The only other noise—
his mumbles to himself
words he can't hear
and the cat mewing on the
wrong side of the door.

Could it be the couple who left Hedley
twenty miles away and came
to fix the old house right,
whose dreams dance through the rooms
at night filling them
with painted colors of hope—
waiting for a future of belonging here
until the apple trees grow
over the back porch?

On a perfect day, when the
wind is low, I'll row across,
between tides. I'll arrive with a shout,
"Hoy to the house, anybody home?"

They'll come out and say,
"You're the house—the one the sun rises on!"

We'll become friends.

Printed with permission

Contents

Preface

"It is Better to Light a Candle than Curse the Darkness"
Chinese Proverb

ather Flanagan had been traveling for awhile and was tired. He had started out later than expected from Boys Town in Omaha, Nebraska, and was arriving late at the Richmond Home for Boys, nestled near the historic Fan District of row houses and small parks. The car ride from downtown had taken him up Main Street past all of the banks and brokerage firms, down the Boulevard until they reached the lake at Byrd Park and around the side of the gardens at Maymont, an old Victorian estate that had been converted into a public park. Everything was quiet.

No one was there to greet him and he could feel his annoyance growing. The night air was still warm from the typical summer heat, hotter than Nebraska at noontime.

It was his first trip to the old orphanage, started back in 1846, now almost a hundred years old, and he had yet to meet the superintendent. The man's name had slipped his mind. He stepped up to the front door of the tall red brick building and beat on the door, calling out for someone to answer.

"Hello? Hello?" he said, trying to sound authoritative, important, to make someone crawl out of their comfortable bed just a little faster and let him in.

The sound of the lock being turned made the old father take a step back and stand up straighter, preparing himself to make a good first impression.

As the door opened he saw only a small boy in thin, cotton pajamas standing in the dim light, one hand still on the handle of the door.

"Who is in charge of this institution?" asked the father, his voice a little too loud.

"This ain't no institution, this is my home," said the boy, drawing himself up just as firmly, letting the father know he had made an enormous mistake.

The father smiled and felt some of the weariness drain from his body.

"Well, then, may I come in?" he asked, his voice softening.

Lore handed down at the Virginia Home for Boys & Girls, Richmond, Virginia.

Introduction

A Little History

> *"The good neighbor looks beyond the external accidents and discerns those inner qualities that make all men human and therefore, brothers."*
>
> **Rev. Martin Luther King Jr., *Strength to Love*, 1963**

There's an old saying that "blood is thicker than water," that biology is what makes a family strong no matter what. That blood ties bury deep within the DNA the need to know who your family is and where they're scattered. But some have a family that grew in their heart and they're on a quest to find them all, many years later.

Frank Szemko has almost sixty brothers and sisters but doesn't know where all but a few of them are anymore. He doesn't even know if they're alive and well or passed away years ago. The Family Tree Project though (at www.sharedabundance.us), part of a national college scholarship foundation where any alumnus of a US orphanage can post

13

old photos, their name, the name of their home, and the years they were there, may finally help him find out.

Frank is an alumnus of the Brooklyn Orphan Asylum Society, now shuttered. Only the building that held the dorms, offices, cafeteria, classrooms—his entire world as a child—still stands. Now it's the offices for the town of Islip. He knows because he lives 500 yards away from the home, his old home.

The history of his life is held within the children he grew up with. They are the ones who know the ending of every childhood story and can laugh easily with him, again, at a once forgotten prank. They are the ones who have known him the longest and can see through any layers he has put on over the years and remind him of how much he has always been loved.

While on his journey he also hopes others who grew up in more traditional definitions of family come to understand what he has always known. His childhood in an orphanage, and thousands of other childhoods like his, were happy ones.

He has grown up with the images pushed upon him of nightmare homes that outsiders have concocted from their imaginations. None of *Annie* or *Oliver!* was ever true for him or the Brookwood home, their nickname for the home. It was a great place to grow up, he says.

They had chores and earned an allowance; they went to the nearby public school and made friends who came by for dinner. The only differences between him and most of us were that there were eight other beds in his room and he ate dinner with sixty other people who didn't really look like Frank.

There was always something to talk about. A huge camaraderie, he says.

And, when he needed to, Frank could turn to any one of the older guys, his big brothers, and ask for help or advice. "They were always there," he says.

The girls and boys of Brookwood knew they were the children of the men and women who worked there, giving their hearts and souls to their well-being. "William Saint-Marie, the director of the children, was a father to me," said Frank. "He had a gift to make every child feel like they mattered and spent time with us putting on puppet shows and building model airplanes. And, if somebody needed to be squared away, they were but nobody ever raised a hand to us." Punishment was walked off around the campus or in time-out.

Alice Ray, the supervisor of the senior boys, wrote Frank every month for years after he left and taught him the ABC's of a date. When he was in the army, he came back to visit her, and the other members of his family at Brookwood, all the time.

"I had to get along with a lot of people from a young age. It opened up my heart more and has made it easier to get to know others, not harder, because I know my family loved me," he said. It is the foundation he has built his life upon, and it has been a good life.

But, time passed and the home closed, and the kids he grew up with moved on to wives and husbands and kids of their own, and they lost touch. He misses them all.

So, two of his "brothers," Wayne and Merrill Higgins, and Frank are determined to search out the other pieces of their family. At the top of Frank's wish list is Julio Quintano, a muscular kid back in the 1940s with a lot of savvy who looked out for all of the younger fellows. Or Bobby Howard. Or Jean Omland. She was Frank's first girlfriend.

Frank's dream is of an enormous family reunion where everyone can trade photos of grandchildren and stories of where they've been and what they've seen. They can see how each other has turned out and cheer each other on or offer a shoulder to those who need it. Like any other family.

He loves them all, and misses them. Maybe soon he will see some of them again.

"Consider the constant cycling of death and rebirth, the endless going and return. Everything you experience has a beginning, a middle and an end, and is followed by a new beginning, therefore do not draw back from the passage into darkness: when in deep water, become a diver."

Ralph H. Blum, *The Book of Runes*

It stands to reason that if some new goo-gaw or invention or scientific discovery was doing a great job, we'd all know about it. After all, this is the age of information overload with text messaging, the Internet, and twenty-four-hour news stations.

But there is an entire movement, centuries old, that is enjoying a comeback and doing a great job at what is deemed by many an intractable problem—and chances are, you don't know about it.

Orphanages, which began in the United States before the American Revolution, are in the middle of a recent resurgence with surprising results. New homes are opening, a dozen are expected soon mostly in the West, and they are welcoming children in ever-increasing numbers.

The story of modern orphanages though, now called residential education facilities (REF), has been largely ignored for over sixty years. Their stories have mostly gone untold.

Not only are they thriving after a radical drop in numbers during the 1980s, they have lessons to offer every parent in America on how to raise our children into happy, confident, independent, and loving adults. Parenting tips are included in appendix B. They are gathered from each home's wisdom to use in your own household. Take what works for you and leave the rest.

But we can only see the blessing they have to offer if we can first put aside the myths and read the stories captured here with an open mind.

A vacuum of information about children's homes has given the myths that have always surrounded orphanages in this country lasting power. Their hold is so secure, few of us have left room for even the possibility that we don't know the truth. We believed the tales of institutionalized children who were kept fed and housed but were deprived of the chance to create familial bonds.

The idea of a nurturing environment and a decent childhood wasn't even a consideration. I was guilty of the same thought. Too many late night dramas that saved another innocent right before they were to be sent off to *the home.*

That point was driven home early in the research of the book when I attempted to write a short editorial about Frank Szemko who grew up at the Brooklyn Orphan Asylum Society in Islip on Long Island, New York, from 1946 to 1951.

I kept interviewing seniors who had grown up in different homes across America who couldn't find the children most referred to as their "brothers and sisters," and the sense of loss they carried was profound.

Frank was representative of the people I'd met. He lives in a house in the shadow of the Brooklyn Society, now a town building, to stay close to the home, his childhood home, because it was the greatest symbol he had left of a childhood he cherished. Living nearby eased the pain of not having enough people to share those memories with—other alumni.

Frank kept most of the stories out of his daily life, where they could have lived again for a little while in their retelling, to avoid the curious questions or outright statements that were benignly rude.

I wrote about Frank's childhood and how much he longed to find the other children, now senior citizens like himself, and submitted it to a nearby large metro paper that had run several editorials before, but this time I ran into a problem.

No matter how hard I tried, the editor, who had no personal experience of any home, including Frank's, couldn't believe Frank's version of events. He flatly refused to believe Frank was telling the truth. At best, Frank had left out details in his old age.

Frank's hurt and anger was palpable, and there was nothing I could offer but the chance to try again. That's why his story, along with those of several alumni from the homes profiled here, is recaptured in short vignettes in between each chapter.

The Family Tree Project, a part of The Shared Abundance Foundation, was started as a result of the alumni of US orphanages who want to find each other. No Internet bulletin board existed so I started posting old photos, the names of the homes, and the years people lived there as a means to help people reconnect. More information about this free service can be found at the foundation's web site at www.shared-abundance.us under The Family Tree Project. More about the foundation is included in appendix A.

My experience with Frank and the editor was just a taste of what was to come. Someone pointed out to me as I set out that this was going to be a very telling journey for me because I was stepping into a place others had obviously chosen not to. Nothing gets ignored by the larger press by mistake for sixty years. There has to be a lot of motivation.

They were right.

The word orphanage raised issues from the start from every quarter. It possesses a radioactive quality that few words not considered *four-letter* possess. Several homes didn't want me to even step foot on their property lest they become tainted with the word—*orphanage.* Several kept reminding me their facility was different, implying their children were somehow different and not to confuse the two. Some homes no longer accept children from social services to avoid the political hammering. However, some social workers have been known to give parents who face losing their child to foster care a choice to take their child and place them in a nearby home before the courts catch up with them. Not all of the parents whose children end up in foster care or at REFs were neglectful parents. Many of them, in fact, were doing the best they could with the resources or circumstances, such as illness or poverty, handed to them.

The REFs' unwillingness to give me access ranged from anger to many phone calls to references to make sure I'd get the story straight before I was allowed entrance. I understood their apprehension; there are over 600,000 reasons—all of America's children in need of a home, who didn't need the myth enlarged or worsened.

But there is also a small, growing movement by older alumni of US orphanages fed up with the ignorance surrounding their childhood who want the word revived and insisted I use only *the word*—orphanage—in conversations and not the longer moniker, residential education facility. To them, that was the insult and a denial of their truth.

Some politicos oppose the entire idea of orphanages, academies, or residential education facilities. There is a campaign in several states to deny any of the hundreds of thousands of dispossessed children in the social service system the right to stay at a residential education facility.

All of that dust was raised after visiting only one home, the Virginia Home for Boys and Girls, which is quietly hidden behind the West Tower Theater on a main thoroughfare of Richmond, Virginia—my hometown.

I was well aware of the movie theater; I had been there many times over the years, but was unaware of the home that stood on a green, wide campus right behind the strip mall. Their story is told in chapter 1, and it will enlighten a lot of people who have driven right by the small sign for years.

And, there is something more their stories have to offer. There's a certain magic for every person who's faced one of life's changes, whether it was divorce, or a death, or a sudden career turn, or even darker stories of addiction or crippling grief or whatever you might be facing. If you've ever wondered, standing at the edge of some change you never really wanted and weren't sure if you should retreat or go forward into the unknown, listen to these stories. You will see a way to believe in your own possibilities and perhaps embrace change in yourself.

That was the unexpected twist in the story for myself and my teenage son, Louie. We became part of the story little by little, our struggles to deal with large changes the same year I began this book. The path didn't start out that way, but became a journey to get me to let go and see the blessings through loss, struggle, and pain and, finally, coming back together for both of us.

There are just three things more to get out of the way before you can dive right into this book and get to know all of us and why I took on this project: Louie and me—these diverse people who have one goal in common, which is to raise healthy, happy children who grow into families of their own makings—and the miraculous story of how Louie and I survived and grew stronger.

The first is that I know a little about what it's like to grow up surrounded by a lot of people you aren't related to, but have to get along with, because I was raised on a campus, the Virginia Theological Seminary in Alexandria, Virginia. My dad, Reverend Dabney Jefferson Carr III, was an Episcopal minister and on the faculty for over twenty years.

It was the 1970s when I grew up there, which is significant because it was a more liberal time, less paranoid, and no color alerts. Civil rights movements were going strong for both people of color and women, and the debates were happening not only in our house but all across the campus. Segregation had recently ended and women were given the right to be ordained in the Episcopal Church. My father had played small, quiet roles in both pageants and took me along on his forays into the struggles a lot of the time. Not to bear witness, but to take part and get to know the details of the people who were determined not to be defined by how others saw them. Not all of it went well.

The church I had grown up in, and my father had devoted his life to, fractured in places and splintered a little with both new ideals. Threats were made against African-American clergy and newly ordained women. They came from both inside the church and without, but my father remained calm, only occasionally shaking his head, before setting out to do what he saw as the right thing: nominating his best friend, Henry Mitchell, the first African-American to graduate from the Virginia Seminary, for a seat on what had been an all-white church board; casting his vote at the Episcopal General Assembly to ordain women; or walking by my side in the march on Washington for the Equal Rights Amendment as I shouted slogans and he looked on, bemused. They were very heady times.

My mother, Leontine, Tina for short, a worrier by trade, occasionally voiced out loud in clear sentences what she spent a lot of time hinting at—that maybe this wasn't going to go well this time—but she never stopped either one of us from going. That's all you can ask sometimes.

The other adults around me, the students and the faculty, believed in the possibilities, which isn't a common trait among most people. A lot of us spend far more time talking about what didn't go right, what isn't going well, and what can't possibly happen. We spend too much time peering into the little window to the inside of the soul letting us know there is mostly fear residing there. But, imagine being brought up with the idea that things will not only be okay, but you don't have to know how all of that will happen. It's another key ingredient to all of these successful residential education facilities, and we'll talk more about that later. It's also something to keep in mind in all families.

What's also important is the people who made up the seminary thought that they had a duty to create bonds and share even with us, the faculty rug rats. There were constant pick-up softball games in the field behind our house or the open green right in front of the main administration buildings. If a faculty member wasn't feeling well or was housebound, somebody's child was sent over just to check in on occasion and see if everything was all right.

The idea that I was connected to all of these different human beings—faces that kept changing from year to year—became ingrained into the definition of what I thought was the way people lived together in a community.

Every week brought communal dinners in the refectory where we mingled with the other kids and got updates on who was doing what. There were endless "oohs" and "aaahs" over accomplishments and words of comfort over what didn't go well. I had endless conversations about how confusing the world of boys was with one of the first women to be ordained, Pat Parks. Pat always did me the honor of taking me seriously and never laughing at why Tommy Vinson didn't know I was alive or fretting about being the tallest girl at 5'9" in the seventh grade. My nickname was stilts and my wild hair and knees were the widest things on me. But when I was talking to Pat I forgot about all of that and felt smart and like I had something to offer. That left a small space within me forever for that idea to grow and blossom.

At the beginning of every new school year when we all gathered together at the refectory and listened to the new seminary students describe their old lives, the kids were listening for which students had the best hobbies, best talents. These were the ones we would cajole into teaching us judo one year, square dancing another, and one year magic tricks. We had a film buff for three years who brought the reels of old movies (this was long before VCRs or DVDs), and we watched *The High and the Mighty* with John Wayne and another time all of *Gone with the Wind* while sitting on the floor of an empty class room. We didn't make a sound, lost in the movie.

Another memorable era, the three years he studied there, a free spirit came to the seminary. His name is lost to me now but I remember his long hair and how he never wore shoes and left every first floor class by the tall windows that stretched along the front of the building. He was also a great magician, which would have been more than enough for me to remember him, but it was his desire to be himself in every situation and allow the same of everyone else that left me with a lasting thought that who we are is important.

That is one of the essential ingredients each of the homes you'll get a glimpse into works to impart to each of the hundreds of children that come through their doors each year.

All of the people at the seminary did the same for us. They went out of their way to make the entire campus body *a family* and to include the children in their care and concern. I never knew what it was like not to have a hundred buttinskis constantly in my life, telling me a thing or two. I knew if I skinned my knee around Aspen Hall it would be bandaged before I made it to the back of the Gibson's house, just across the road from the back of my house. I might not know who would be there to help, but I knew someone would reach out. It was a different definition of family but for me, it was normal.

My definition of home didn't consist of the split-level house we actually lived in because I always knew it wasn't really ours. It was the Seminary's and would be passed to another family as soon as we were gone.

My home consisted of that house, the large field in front, the rolling hills right behind it, the gym, the refectory, the library, the dorms, the tennis courts, and the small ancient post office. The postmistress there prided herself on knowing which family you were from just by looking at you and was always telling me how wonderful we all were. I took her into my heart as one of us because of the attitude she brought to the table.

It was every building, every hillside, every tree, *and* every person who lived there year after year. That's how I defined family.

Save the arguments that say I still had an intact nuclear family to return home to because that's an obvious ideal. No one is saying to give up on trying to heal individual families through wrap-around care or find new families through adoption; only that home has many definitions and when "ideal" no longer exists, growing up on a campus is not so bad and sometimes can be really wonderful. And, as you'll see as you visit each of the homes captured in these pages, there is plenty of nurturing going on there as well.

My father, a very funny man who never met a stranger, was well-loved and knew it, is now buried at the Seminary next to Henry, his old friend. When I go to visit my father's grave it's unavoidable that I get stopped, even now, by some more buttinskis wanting to know how I am, what am I up to, and there are a few hugs. They are still my family and like a lot of the kids you're going to meet in this book, when I think of family I think of all of them.

Dad was still alive when the possibilities of this book began. This is the second useful thing to know, because I started this book with a life that went in one direction, and before I could even write the first words it was taking off at a rapid pace in another, whether I liked it or not. I didn't know when I started out, but meeting all of these people was going to teach me far more than I knew at the time and would play a bigger part in the large changes I was about to face. It would play a part in the choices I'd have to make.

I had been taking care of my father for well over a year, nursing him back from an illness that had left him unable to move. My three sisters and brother helped out a lot as well, but due to close quarters and by now routine, it was my father and I who spent the most time together, giving us the chance to wrestle a few unexpected blessings out of the whole ordeal.

We had lived together, my parents, my son, and me for fifteen years in a small, red brick ranch house on a quiet cul-de-sac in the west end of Richmond, Virginia. It was a safe existence with calculated challenges. It was all I told myself I was capable of handling if I was going to successfully figure out how to raise a child on my own and figure out a career as a writer. I had limited the possibilities down to a very short list to ensure against failure, and to ensure against somehow inexplicably harming my year-old son without even knowing I was doing it. I was running from the end of an abusive marriage and had come to a place at twenty-nine years old when I entered the front door of my parents' new home—what was supposed to be their retirement nest—with the idea that I was incapable of figuring anything out successfully. A lot had happened and I had forgotten, at least for a while, the lessons of my childhood and was in need of a different story.

Fairy tales are stories that start out in dire circumstances and maybe along the way appear to break the spirit of all the good people wrapped up inside of them. But we keep reading them because eventually, we know for certain, it'll all be okay, and every once in a while that's exactly what we need. To know ahead of time everything will be okay. That's what I needed back then, to know ahead of time I was safe and nothing else could go wrong before I was going to be willing to try. Try anything. I wanted my own fairy tale.

Louie, my perfect child who seemed imperfect to the world, snapped me out of that. Louie taught me at long last how to live. He's still doing that because, even now, I can be a reluctant listener. But it was also going to take all the lessons of each home I was going to visit to put all of the pieces together.

I don't need the fairy tales anymore, thanks to my year-long adventure, but that's part of the story I'm going to tell you. How I got there and what we had to go through. Now that's a twisted tale.

For Louie and me, everything happened in a backward motion. I found out about the child before I was married, before I knew who I was or what I wanted to really do with the rest of my life. The child came first, and probably had to if I was ever going to have any faith in myself. I had come to a place at twenty-seven years old where I felt unsure about every step and knew with certainty everything I had would eventually ebb away. I never put too much attachment on anything.

But then the idea of this child became real and everything changed.

It was April 1, 1987, and I was sitting on a gurney in a makeshift Doc-in-the-Box. Every cubicle was separated by pale green gathered sheets, and I'd been waiting a while with no dated magazines, no charts of horrible diseases to study. I was there because I was worried I had the beginnings of an ulcer.

A young doctor stepped into the cubicle next to mine and I eavesdropped out of boredom, listening to a girl flirt with the doctor.

I still saw myself as a girl then; unformed, dependent, and completely at loose ends. My entire life description could change at will and it would have been okay.

She was giggling as he asked her if she was on any birth control pill. The antibiotic would cancel it out, he told her. Never heard that one before. It probably said it on the folded paper inside each pack, but no, I didn't read them. That was when the idea first entered my consciousness. The idea of a child—but even then it was only a glance, not a real thought.

It was finally my turn and the well-scrubbed face from the next cubicle, no older than mine, nervously told me the results of one of the tests he'd taken. He spit it out quickly. "You're pregnant."

I smiled for a moment, and his face relaxed a little. "Okay, not so bad?" he asked. "You smiled, that was your first reaction." He was worried about me. Worried I was thinking about the chain reaction of disasters this was already starting for a young single woman. He was trying to calm me down. But from the moment the child became real I was already changing into something else.

I was already thinking my life had been saved. What I couldn't do for myself I would do for this new being. This child would be my excuse to try, to survive. I was just about out of ideas otherwise.

I took the small white square of plastic with a pale blue 'x' in the center of it home to show the prospective father. Before we knew it he would quickly fade from our lives for the most part and leave me and this child, gratefully, to our own devices. The marriage would turn out to be violent and brutal and I would spend too much of my time trying to fix it. He would suggest often that if I only lost weight, even though I was thin, or cleaned house better, even though it was clean, he would love us. I believed him and tried to do what I could to fix the situation. It never worked and there would be threats or a fist, maybe some shoving. But that was all to come.

At this place in time this man and I were engaged with invitations in the mail for a June wedding and all that that encompassed. I knew that wasn't meant to last either but I wanted to be able to say I had at one time been married. I had sunk so far back inside of myself that I thought only someone who needed help worse than I did would be willing to hitch up with me. At the time, maybe it was true.

I was taking part in a bigger disaster than I knew right there, on that day, but I was determined and it would be short-lived, so, no looking back.

He was sitting on the couch of the small house he rented when I came in through the back. He was watching a game on TV, ignoring me till I spoke up.

"I'm pregnant," I said, from across the room. No segue, no conversation to lead him in the direction we were headed. I was living in my own world already and not thinking about him.

He immediately started laughing, hard.

"That's the best one I've heard all day," he said, slapping his knee. It was April Fools Day. I had forgotten. He was starting to go into a long list of jokes people had tried to pull on him, all unsuccessful, waving his arms and laughing. As he was talking I held out my hand and let my fingers unwrap from around the blue 'x'. It had been in my hand for hours. It was my tangible proof of my own newly found importance.

He stopped laughing, stopped moving. He didn't need to get any closer to make sure of what it was. He knew, but I'm not sure I really cared what he thought.

"I'm going to leave you alone right now so you don't say anything we'll both have to remember forever," I said. I'll tell the truth here, though, because that wasn't it. I didn't really care what he thought, not at this point. I didn't want him taking away pieces of what I'd found. He'd try often enough in the year ahead, but for that moment, the joy of being saved was all mine. It had taken me twenty-seven years to come to a place I wasn't going to be budged from. I was going to enjoy it, at least for that day.

We got quietly married on April twenty-first in a hastily thrown-together wedding at his rented house. The justice of the peace had badly stained teeth and a comb-over, and he wore a lime green double-knit jacket and a shiny gold tie. There was no family present but, somehow, everyone we called had managed to get there. Amy brought flowers; Vic wore his tux and brought a camera. A sheet cake appeared along with sparkling cider and champagne.

We stood on the sundeck of his house amidst twenty-or-so friends at right around dinner time as neighbors craned over privacy fences to see what we were doing.

During the vows I started laughing; loud laughing, almost guffaws that wouldn't stop. The justice of the peace knew enough to keep going and I said 'I do' in the middle of a laugh while I watched a neighbor push a lawn mower around his small square of a yard. The whole thing struck me as absurd and more of a requirement to please others than to live happily ever after. I wasn't thinking that far ahead.

My new husband decided we shouldn't tell his family and to go ahead with the June wedding as planned. I'd march down the aisle, very pregnant in my mother's altered wedding dress that she'd bought off the rack at J.C. Penney in 1947 and her veil, and it'd be like we weren't already hitched. For some reason, no one questioned the idea and for two months I did my best to remember who knew me as married and who didn't.

Six months later Louie was born five weeks early on a Friday morning. He was perfect, covered in fine hair and the white, sticky film of a preemie with patches of pink skin showing through where the midwife had hastily swiped with a cloth. Ten fingers, ten toes, a perfect, round mole on his bottom and on his head a crop of orange-red curly hair and bright blue eyes.

"I'm glad you're here," I said, "and I'll always watch over you and keep you safe." Moments later he stopped breathing.

While the doctors and nurses had been quietly and furiously working on Louie I had been slowly bleeding out right behind them. The noise in my head was growing to a roar and I could barely hear what anyone was saying.

"So this is what they mean by 'ringing in your ears,'" I said, completely unalarmed, marveling at the experience.

A heavyset nurse with deep brown skin turned and looked at me with an expression of surprise and alarm, staring at my happy face. The nurses quickly split into two groups—one for Louie and one for me; both of us unaware the other was in trouble.

Louie was whisked away and I wouldn't see him again till the evening. He was my first and was to be my only child, and I had no idea he stood on the edge for a while, deciding whether to stay or to go.

When they whisked him out of the room, they rushed him to the Neonatal Intensive Care Unit (NICU) where he was resuscitated and placed in an incubator. No one told us anything until after he was stable again. I was grateful I had missed the chance to wonder if it was all going to end before it had really gotten started. I was already hanging on to motherhood as a way to save myself, to form a whole person.

"Boy, was he dusky," said the pediatrician on call, an older man with no bedside manner. Louie's color had changed from pink to a deep rose as the oxygen in his small new body declined, but by the time I saw him again he was pink, with attachments.

The two of us would end up staying in the hospital together, right across the hall from each other. Louie had been premature, but large at 8 pounds, 12 ounces. The obstetrician, Dr. Maizels, my old friend Max, said he would have more likely been 12 pounds if he'd gone full term.

Early on, in order to be near Louie, I was going to have to come to the NICU and carefully lift him out of his incubator, maneuvering around the IV that was now in his small arm and withstand the plaintiff cries when they pricked his heel every hour.

I loved him fiercely already. I've heard mothers say it took them a little while to bond with their new baby, but not me. I felt a connection to him so strong I was convinced he could understand me without my saying a word. I believed it so firmly I risked breaking a WASP rule of always sticking to the empirical, the concrete, and told an old friend of my new language between Louie and me. She looked tolerant but not very impressed and a little shocked. I kept it to myself after that but cherished the new talent.

"His insulin levels are still a little high," a nurse mentioned to me. "He'll be fine, but it could cause learning disabilities when he's older."

She wasn't even really speaking to me as much as she was handing out tidbits of information, passing the time. I didn't care, anyway. School was a long way off and I wanted to hold my child without so much help or advice. I wanted to be his mother and figure out what that meant.

"Come see the big red-headed baby over here," I heard a young father say, waving over his robed wife from the regular nursery window. There was Louie in an incubator with his bright red curls, and a crowd of people already curious about him.

All of the other babies in the NICU were smaller at three and five pounds, but healthier and had already been there for a while, some for months. The parents would glide in, looking rested and well-dressed. I watched them, wearing my yellow sear-sucker robe over a hospital gown, my skin still the color of oatmeal, and marveled at how calm they looked, how in control. I knew they had a plan for every footstep, every motion they made.

It wasn't until almost two weeks later that Louie was deemed healthy enough to go home, and the doctors had decided they couldn't explain an irregular heartbeat I had and wanted to let me go anyway. I went along with whatever they were saying as long as I was going to be able to take Louie home.

Louie was wheeled in a bassinet into my room. We were alone at last.

I felt unsure of myself as I tried my best to dress him in the small outfit I had picked out for taking him home. A store-bought fussy white outfit with blue trim and a yellow cable-knit sweater my mother had made with a matching cap.

It took five of us to figure out how to put him into the new car seat, and it would be days later before we figured out how to connect the car seat to the car. We drove home slowly, my hand steadying the seat, on a warmer than usual November day to the north side of Richmond, Virginia, and started a new life.

"He looks like you spit him out," said an old woman, a neighbor who had grown up in the country. The neighbors had all gathered around to get a good look at the new baby.

She was right, with every day that passed Louie looked more and more like a small, male version of me. He would be perpetually tall for his age with strawberry blonde curly hair that slowly took the place of the orange crown, with deep blue eyes and a small Gaelic nose.

His father's strong Italian features with a prominent Roman nose made him look like a stranger holding his own baby.

It took less than a year for the marriage to finally disintegrate under its own weight amid the abuse. He left during his lunch hour saying he didn't want to miss time at work.

I had already taken Louie to my parents and the seminary, to my old home, the week before for safekeeping. I was always willing to risk my own well-being, but I had found a boundary—Louie.

"I married you because you had money and now you don't, so I'm leaving," he said, as he pulled the door behind him. I stood in the living room of our small yellow stucco house feeling the vacuum of his abandonment. I was grateful for it, but I'd never had an illusion collapse so completely on me before.

After Louie and I were left alone in the house on Elmsmere Avenue, I discovered that none of the bills had been paid for three months and any grace periods I might have gotten were passed. No job, no money, time to go.

I sold the house, packed up everything we owned, and we moved to a small town on the Rappahannock River, Tappahannock, Virginia, for a new career as a writer. I was making my own path, against everyone else's ideas of who I should be or what I should want.

My family, or *The Family*, as I thought of them then, was an old Virginia family of famous names, a past president, governors, and diplomats who were used to getting involved in each other's business and helping to decide what was best. I was straying.

They gathered together to try and figure out how to put me back on their path. My well-intentioned younger brother, a newly minted lawyer, was chosen as the one to cajole me into career counseling. After two days of endless questions, the results said I would make a good minister or writer. *The Family* did not try to hide its disappointment.

"Didn't it say anything else?" my brother asked, anguished at my prospects.

"No," I said, feeling an edge of freedom, wondering what to do next. I wasn't used to being acknowledged as right, even if it was given grudgingly from a test.

Everyone was flummoxed. It was generally agreed I'd drown and possibly take Louie with me. They seemed completely unaware I'd been drowning right underneath their noses for years.

"Become a secretary," my father pronounced, as he often did when he thought he certainly knew better and wasn't in the mood for a discussion.

"No," I said, realizing it would lead nowhere for me and I'd done enough of that already from every angle. He looked stricken. I was surprised too. I'd spoken up and stuck to it.

I hadn't spent enough time saying no. Early on I'd been labeled as opinionated and stubborn. To get along I tried going along way too much. It would take me a very long time to figure out the definition of opinionated for a southern woman is having an opinion that isn't handed to me.

I got a job at a small weekly newspaper in Tappahannock, the *Rappahannock Times*. The biggest news story while I was there was about the two cars involved in a head-on fender bender right in front of the paper's building.

"Thanks for being convenient," I said, once I was sure no one was even bruised. I was often on the verge of getting yelled at by someone because of something I'd said.

Once I mistakenly wrote an obituary about an elderly Baptist minister who wasn't dead yet, prompting a lot of anguished phone calls and an appearance by the family, demanding a retraction. We were happy to do it and I cautiously pointed out how heartening it was to see how many people were going to eventually miss the man.

Louie and I rented out the temporarily empty parsonage, right next to the cemetery and behind the church, two blocks from the river and one block from the private boarding school, St. Margaret's Episcopal Girls High School.

A female member of the faculty told me shortly after I arrived not to put down any roots there and get out as quickly as possible.

"A single woman could rot here," she whispered. That's not my biggest worry, I thought. And I was already rotting from the inside out, but ignoring it.

Louie and I often walked barefoot down to the small beach at the end of our street, past the two blocks of downtown Tappahannock that lined both sides of the street, to the river to play in the surf. Louie, not yet two, was born unafraid of anything and was constantly throwing himself off of the couch, trying to climb everything, wedging himself into tight corners, and running into the river with open arms. The river ran up to greet him and bowled him over backward every time, turning him end to end till he washed up on the shore at my feet.

Others at the beach tried to keep an eye on both of us, watching Louie go through the spin cycle of the Rappahannock while I stood calmly on the edge of the water waiting for him to quickly surface. Louie loved the river and would pop up out of the water smiling, gasping for air, his bathing suit hanging on to the edge of a wet diaper. People glanced at me nervously as I scooped up a wet, wriggling Louie, anxious to get back to the water. I smiled in their direction but never offered an explanation. I knew the river couldn't take him far and Louie was in his element, unsure of what was going to happen next but thrilled at the ride. That was Louie.

I envied his ability to throw himself into anything without caution and be happy with whatever happened. I was constantly being forced into the same kind of deal but without the ability to be happy without first knowing the outcome. And, of course, I could never know what was to come, but I was always making attempts at controlling it.

For some reason, though, in our little house in Tappahannock it was just a bit easier to live. I kept the back door of our house unlocked all the time without a worry and came home to find a bag of still-warm tomatoes from someone's garden or a small plate of lemon squares with a note. I remember being in the kitchen and looking up in time to see a long procession of young women, all dressed in fancy white dresses and small white gloves go past the house on their way from the church back to the school. It was like living in a safe, dreamy world and was a perfect womb for me, for a while.

But Tappahannock could only hold us for so long. The job at the newspaper had never really paid enough and the savings from the sale of the yellow stucco house were running out. I needed to find somewhere else to go. I was tired though of trying to figure things out.

There was one exception, one person, though to whom I always tried to give everything I had; that was Louie.

For everyone who believes that families who end up working with a residential education facility must have been neglectful, must not have cared enough, must not have had resources, pay attention to how my story began. You will come to the understanding that the wall between the suburbs and the homes like the ones in this book are very thin at times and a good number of these children have loving parents trying to do the best they can.

I loved Louie unabashedly from the start and did everything by instinct, ignoring all the rules people tried to shove at me, in protest of what I was already bearing on my soul.

He had everything he might want. As the first grandchild, my sisters and brother and family galore with all of that pent-up baby energy showered him with toys and books and love and affection. Louie was magical from the start.

He danced to music only he could hear and I fell in step, catching the rhythm from his movements and boogying down a grocery aisle in the Food Lion right behind him. He approached groups of strangers on our little beach and started babbling, smiling broadly, easily charming all of them. I'd let him, following behind, grateful to have figured out an introduction that didn't require me to go first.

When I was with him, I was peaceful in a simple way I hadn't been since I was small. Louie could be different and I was happily following him, mimicking his behavior, learning how to *be*.

It was time to leave Tappahannock though, and be back among the weeds of family and expectations. A sense of dread accompanied the move but perhaps the only way to finally figure out anything was to plow right straight through the middle of it. I didn't know.

I packed everything back up, left our little house in Tappahannock and took Louie to Charlottesville for three months for a short-lived job, before heading back to Richmond, stumbling into figuring out a plan, taking it day by day, forging a different kind of life than any of my four siblings had ever known. I was imploding on the inside; surviving the marriage had exposed how little I knew about myself, but I was determined to figure it out for Louie's sake. What I would never do for myself, I would do for my child. For years that one idea saved my life.

I arrived on the doorstep of my parents newly owned red brick ranch house, the first home they had ever owned, with no place else to go, a career still in the earliest stages that no one thought was a good idea, and their only grandchild.

Louie was born early on a Friday morning, October 30, 1987, the first day of his life and the first day I even considered letting myself have one. Most people would say this is where their new life began. But

I had such a long way to go till that day. The world was going to expend a lot of energy telling me what was wrong with Louie, his unseen problems that were causing them problems. But they had it wrong. Louie was perfect from the beginning. He was going to teach me how to see the same thing in myself, and then maybe, I'd get a chance to live too. I didn't feel ready, but with Louie, I was willing to take a chance.

For Louie I would try, and the world, the one that likes to keep everything neat and orderly and would be bothered by Louie, was going to force me into trying. Thank God for that world, thank God for Louie. Thank God for the homes that would help me when we would suddenly need it the most, when everything suddenly changed.

Even in the suburbs, hidden from view, change found me anyway. As I kept writing, looking for an idea for a new book, my father became very ill and needed someone to watch over him. After a long stint in a rehabilitation hospital he came home and lay across the hall from where I sat and worked, listening to me make phone calls and type. I knew he was there, listening, and I wandered across that short distance every so often to help him change clothes or fetch a dropped hearing aid or a glass of water.

The spaces between *doing* were filled by my father mostly, with stories of growing up in Richmond without a father. His father, Cary, had become bed-ridden with lung cancer when my father was seven and passed away when Dad was only nine. After that, most of the bigger decisions in my father's life were up to him—and I discovered he was as uncomfortable about making any of them as I was now.

"You know, when I didn't finish high school with my class, your grandmother kicked me out. I ended up renting a room I shared with another man," he explained one afternoon as I changed the sheets on his bed. He watched from his wheelchair. Who knows why he picked this story to tell, and after all these years of never letting these details slip out. I listened intently as I made a neat, tight hospital corner—just the way both of us liked a bed to be made.

"I dug ditches to pay for the room, so did my roommate. At the end of the week when we got paid I watched all of the other men use their paychecks to buy beer and cigarettes and I knew if I didn't change something I was never going to get any further than right there. It scared me to death."

I looked up from the bed but didn't say a word. I knew he was trying to let me know I had waited long enough to set out.

My son Louie, only sixteen, helped carry his grandfather back and forth to the shower, or down the front steps to be gently placed in the car. Watching my son care for his grandfather felt as if I was witness to a love made visible that is made stronger in moments of vulnerability.

Louie had grown up in that house and thought of my father as his own. They had a million private jokes between them and thought of each other as "the greatest." When Dad was at his weakest moment in the intensive care unit, and living was going to take some conscious effort on his part as pumps helped his heart beat and his lungs breathe, Louie had grown so nervous he jumped at Dad, startling him—to make sure he wouldn't give up the ghost too easily.

Later, when Dad was well enough to move with some effort he winked at me, struggled to raise his arms and softly whispered, "Boo!"

In the midst of life moving ahead I kept writing editorials and was still casting around for an idea for a book. A cousin passed along an email from an old friend about an orphanage far away in Rwanda, located in east Africa near the great lakes, looking for boys' underwear and pens.

The request was so simple it became impossible to ignore. The Imbabazi orphanage in Gisenyi, Rwanda, was looking for donations of boys' underwear, any size, and blue or black pens, no pencils. It was a request to help return some piece of normalcy to children who witnessed the slaughter of their parents, neighbors, and friends, making them into orphans.

Normally, I stay out of passing along requests for donations to causes—mostly because the list never ends, and people gravitate to those things they have a natural connection to without my help. But, underwear and pens, it was an almost ridiculous request. And as I stood in the aisle at Wal-Mart picking out boys briefs I thought about all of the school shopping I've done over the years to get my son, Louie, by then a tall seventeen-year-old, ready for his first day of a new grade. The request felt more like a plea from one mother to the next to please help.

I called all of my friends and they chipped in, dropping off boxes of ballpoint pens and packs of briefs in different colors. They all got it. In the absence of hundreds of mothers we would fill in, just a little, with underwear and pens.

The boys and girls were gathered together by a white American elderly woman, Rosamond Carr (no relation) at her home in Gisenyi that she quickly turned into the children's home and school.

The seventy-nine boys and forty-four girls at Imbabazi escaped death in 1994 during the hundred days it takes to pass a season when a mob of Hutus armed mostly with machetes killed over 800,000 human beings, over 10 percent of the population, at a faster clip than the Holocaust. The killing spree specifically targeted Tutsi children in an effort to wipe out the next generation of neighbors and coworkers. The river was so filled with blood it was reported that it became a deep, muddy red visible from a distance.

It was a form of genocide carried out by Hutus as their own darker version of Dr. Seuss' story of Sneetches, killing off the Tutsis who were seen as more desirable.

What was needed was the gathering of voices, of parents everywhere to speak out for the children. And, it's necessary here for the more than 600,000 children in the United States who are in need of a stable home-life. The story of the children at Imbabazi inspired others to encourage me to tell the story of America's children and the blessings of residential education facilities.

If we all gather our voices together and support what already exists, the residential education facilities, the homes, we can help them flourish and give more children a safe place to grow and thrive.

Appendix C includes a list of some of the residential education facilities throughout the United States, along with the Imbabazi orphanage in Rwanda, and the umbrella organization, CORE, and how you can help. During my research of this book, Rosamond passed away peacefully at ninety-four and is buried in her garden at the orphanage, forever with her children.

The third and last thing to know going in, is that orphanages have evolved in the same way families have over the past two hundred years.

The prevailing theories for over a hundred years on child rearing leaned toward duty and obligation and children performed numerous chores, such as tending farm animals, that often helped to contribute to the bottom line. It wasn't the ideal loving home of two parents but as the alumni of these homes continually pointed out to me, with some rancor at those who say otherwise, that they were good years and helped make them into someone they can be proud of.

Most of the children in the homes, though, weren't orphans as portrayed in the popular musicals, *Annie* or *Oliver!*, without a living parent. Most were social orphans who still had a mother or father and were delivered to a home because of hard economic times, abuse, addictions, or neglect. Some were even later reclaimed when conditions improved. It's often the same today.

But orphanages were still seen as cold, gray institutions that had too much in common with prisons. Popular culture helped out with countless books, and then in later years, television shows full of lawyers sending away helpless children into the maw of unforgiving, unloving workers. That's the myopic picture we're still operating with today.

The first shift away from the idea of orphanages began with the orphan trains that ran from 1854 to 1929 sending over 150,000 children from the streets of New York City to midwest and western farms, mostly to farmers needing extra hands. The trains were the obsession of a young minister, Charles Loring Brace, who came from a prominent family in Connecticut to study at a seminary in New York City.

At the time thousands of children were roaming the streets of the city and were given the nickname of "street Arabs." They sold matches, rags, and newspapers to survive along with petty theft and other misdemeanors, which is in part how Brace was able to get support for his idea to send children to what he hoped would be loving families. It was an enormous amount of naiveté, Brace's, crashing into a political headache. The good citizens of New York wanted the problem of children roaming the streets dealt with, but how to do it without appearing cold-hearted or heavy-handed?

Brace founded the Children's Aid Society in 1853 to obtain access to the necessary sources, funding, and transportation to begin the great migration of America's inner city children. The New York Foundling Hospital joined in the project sending unwanted infants as well. Both institutions are still in operation today aiding children.

The operation was casual at best. Children were tagged with their basic information and accompanied by a placing agent. At each stop the children were paraded out onto the train platform where waiting families, who had been notified of the cause and the arrival by handbills, would inspect the children and choose from the selection.

Some families came with good intentions and the result was a new, loving family. Governor Andrew Burke of North Dakota and Governor John Brady of Alaska were both orphan train boys. Governor Brady's fare was paid for by Theodore Roosevelt, Senior, a New York philanthropist and father of the twenty-sixth president of the same name. Brady was so grateful for the new family he later repaid the senior Roosevelt and as governor sought out his son, Theodore Roosevelt, and thanked him.

However, many other children found a different experience as they were inspected for their muscle tone and people peered closely at their teeth. There was no filtering process, no background checks, no questions asked about motives. And not all stories were successes as Billy the Kid was also an orphan train boy.

As the orphan trains faded away, and as children's societies, run mostly by women's and religious charities, were operating close to a thousand orphanages with an estimated 100,000 children who spent on average four years in a home, politicians stepped in with a new idea—foster care.

For many years, there was a belief that a fostering program, an organized form of placing children in private homes, was necessary. The campaign resulted in the 1909 White House Conference on the Care of Dependent Children, chaired by President Theodore Roosevelt. As a result of the conference a shift began away from orphanages, seen as an antiquated and backward solution, and toward individual placement of children into private homes.

However, foster care has not succeeded as well as the Conference of 1909 had hoped. It should be said clearly that foster care parents are the angels on earth who give of themselves to children who are desperately in need of more than just a home. Unfortunately, in the intervening years fewer and fewer families have opened their doors while the number of children in need has doubled since 1986 and continues to grow.

And, there are statistics piling up that show there is a disconnect somewhere in the system that is leaving too many of the children without the necessary life skills they'll need as adults.

According to a year-long project released in 2002 by National Public Radio called Housing First, every year there are 20,000 children who age out of the system and one in four will end up homeless. Half will be unemployed and only half will have graduated from high school.[1] And, according to the National Foster Parent Association,[2] foster care suc-

---

1. www.npr.org/news/specials/housingfirst
2. http://www.nfpainc.org/

ceeds at keeping siblings together only one-fourth of the time, which contradicts the basic principle of preserving the idea of family.

The twist is that children's homes, which have been seen by some as the last option, are doing the job of raising America's children with fewer public dollars than foster care, providing more wrap-around services, and for the homes that belong to the coalition for residential education, CORE, sending more of their kids to college than the general population, according to CORE,[3] without the front-cover fanfare that usually accompanies the near-impossible.

What's more, they're doing it successfully under burdensome federal and state regulations, unmatched by any other child welfare programs while being attacked by a handful of special interest groups that have used the misconceptions about the homes to their advantage. Our collective ignorance is harming a proven solution.

Georgia, for example, is on the verge of passing legislation that no child in its child welfare system can be placed in a residential education facility. It would also require every child placed in foster care be within fifty miles of the home they were removed from. A workable idea for children from the larger cities such as Atlanta, but a little trickier for Georgia's vast rural areas where there are far fewer houses and fewer foster care homes. The reasoning behind the bill is that each child deserves something better—a healthy, single-family home with two caring parents. How true.

But in the meantime the number of children in Georgia who are maturing out of the system into an uncertain adulthood without the skills to navigate socially or economically grows. The bill is the equivalent of refusing any job, even a good one with promise, because it just isn't the ideal one in our imaginations. For some reason, it's only issues surrounding our children that make us completely abandon the pragmatic for the ideal, rather than blending the two for the sake of the children who are waiting for us to behave responsibly.

---

3. http://www.residentialeducation.org/new/index.html

Meanwhile time passes, the situation worsens, and the solutions become more complicated. While foster care does not currently keep statistics on the children that come under its care, the residential education facilities track the children that come into their care—before, during, and after their care. According to a study by Chapin Hall,[4] the Center for Children at the University of Chicago, children placed in residential care in 2003 in the state of Illinois by social services had an average of nine foster care placements prior to arriving at a children's home. Over a third had experienced eleven placements.

The realization that children who come from social services into residential education facilities have suffered an average of five foster care placements, according to anecdotal evidence by advocates inside the homes, but are still nurtured into responsible, caring, independent adults is a story any parent of a slacker teenager would like to hear. Step by step details on how to pull off the same magic trick in their own homes would be nice as well. And that's the best part.

The lessons of modern US orphanages are transferable to the millions of homes whose adults are watching *The Nanny* trying to figure out how to get their child to straighten up and fly right.

We don't need to be trying to fix what isn't broken. There's an opportunity here to listen, learn, and gain something for ourselves. It's what I was going to need that year I visited the homes in order to save first myself and then offer something to Louie.

There's an old saying passed around by parents that goes, just when you get the knack of how to raise the first child, the second one comes along and teaches you how little you know. It's a common theme: the idea that taking children successfully from birth to adulthood has so much mystery involved.

It's a miracle any of us turned out halfway decent.

It's also a myth, being undone across the country on campuses dotted with cottages and dorms.

---

4. http://www.about.chapinhall.org/press/newsalerts/2004/ResidentialCare.html

As the evidence has mounted that foster care isn't working well enough to handle the increasing flow of children and residential education facilities are showing success, more homes have quietly begun to open. The Happy Hill Farm Academy in Fort Worth, Texas, was started by a Baptist minister, Ed Shipman, who couldn't find a foster home for two girls in need and stepped into the breach. Thirty-one years later, the home is thriving and growing. Or the Virginia Home for Boys and Girls that recently opened twelve new cottages and a new school and has been in operation for over a hundred years, quietly tucked away on a busy Richmond thoroughfare in the middle of a growing suburb. Or the San Pasquale Academy in San Diego, California, that only accepts foster children who are wards of the state and was started by Judge Milliken, who was tired of watching parents make excuses and abandoning their children for the street. He worked on opening a home modeled after an upscale boarding school; at the same time the youth felony rate in his county dropped from 4,900 in 1997 to 2,300 in 2000.

Quietly ignoring the bad press, not waiting for something better before starting at all, homes around the country have been building scholarship funds, moving away from dorms to individual cottages with teaching parents, or calling themselves academies modeled after boarding schools. The people who work at the homes have carried on and provided the flute lessons and carpooling to football practices and sat in the audiences of countless school plays while giving structure, balance, guidance, and even love to what has become generations of children.

But there are still lists of children they have to turn away because there aren't enough beds, yet.

If you haven't visited what is now called a residential education facility, you don't know what these children's lives are like; but turn the page, the story's about to begin and you're about to find out. And, somewhere in here you may find the road map for your own life as well. Unexpectedly, Louie and I did, too.

Chapter 1

A Definition of Home

The story of the Virginia Home for Boys & Girls, Richmond, Virginia, founded in April 27, 1846, by the Female Humane Association

JOHN'S STORY

"I love the man that can smile in trouble; that can gather strength from distress, and grow brave by reflection."

Thomas Paine

*S*ometimes it's necessary when telling someone's backstory to frame the details in the era that contained their life. The politics that surrounded the person pushed so much into everyday life that a different pall is cast over everything and can even change circumstances.

That is what happened to John Salgado in 1956 as a five-year-old child in Newport News, Virginia. His mother was an American citizen and his father was Portuguese and a restaurant owner. That year his father was caught selling pints of liquor to sailors after-hours and was quickly deported back to Portugal, leaving John and his younger brother alone with their mother and no visible means of support. The state stepped in and suddenly John was living in Richmond at what was then called Richmond Home for Boys, at their older location.

John, who is now fifty-six years old, believes the Jim Crow attitudes of the 1950s South influenced the sentence handed down to his father and then affected his outcome as well. It's an accident of fate that this is where things began to steadily improve.

As a small boy of five he was driven by his grandmother to Richmond. "I remember a whole lot of boys playing ball outside. It was kind of like going to camp kind of thing. But I woke up the next day looking for my grandmother and couldn't find her and was a little mad at that," said John, really working an understatement. His grandmother petitioned the courts and was awarded custody of his younger brother while his mother slipped into a deep depression and alcohol abuse after the loss of her children and spent years in and out of Virginia mental institutions. While in an institution, she was sterilized at the behest of the state, which wasn't discovered by her family till years later when the scandal was exposed. Another footnote to the politics of the time for people who didn't have an equal voice.

However, from here John's story took a different and eventually better turn. The following year in 1957 the home moved to its present address off Broad Street and, at six years old, John was the first person to break ground at a ceremony marking the occasion. As he grew he continued to struggle with his heritage—failing first and second grade the first times in part, he believes, because he mixed Portuguese with English—but eventually he began to settle in and by high school was taking advanced placement courses at nearby Tucker High School. By the time he was twelve, his father had returned to the states and after working for a few years had sought John out, showing up one day at a basketball game. "I noticed a man walk around the side of the dining hall, older guy, and not one of these guys from this country, dressed differently, so you notice all that. And he comes around and asks me, 'Do you know where I can find John Selgado?' and I said, 'Well, that's me.'" They had the opportunity to reconnect, get to know each other.

John's father, along with his grandmother, sued the state for custody of his son, to try and bring John back to Newport News where he had been spending summers and holidays.

But both of them lost.

The judge in the case awarded custody to the home, which John had grown to love. "I agreed with the judge. I was given a middle class upbringing," he said, proud of his past. "The home is one of the best in the country. They do a great job and they've been doing it a long time. Some of the people I grew up with are closer to me than my actual brother."

His fondest memory of the home is actually the first time he returned in 1972, two years after he left for New York City to get to know his father. He had just bought a new car and arrived back in Richmond just as all of the residents were eating dinner. "I parked my car outside and I was walking into the dining hall..." He chokes up momentarily, apologizing and working to regain himself, still moved by the bonds he holds with the family he has at the home. "Many of the guys stood up and clapped," he said, getting the words out in a tumble. "When I graduated from Tucker High School in 1970 the cheers for me going up to get my diploma were near twice as loud as for the other guys going up to get their diplomas," he said, in a soft Virginia drawl.

He tells each story pulled from memory with obvious pride, not only in himself but in the people that raised him. But, what's more telling is what he ended up doing with his life and the pull he felt to go back to his roots—to his home.

After awhile, John convinced his bride, Deborah, (together now for thirty-six years), to move back to Virginia with him where he started a business named for his adopted family, The Richmond Homes Concrete and Construction Company. He found a house for his family directly behind the home, even sharing the same house number— 8716—just one block apart. In 2006 John served as head of the home's alumni association. He's built a good life and passed it along to his daughter, Dawn Marie, recently married and pursuing a doctorate in psychology. And, throughout all of the stories he has drawn together to make up his history, the details that surrounded him, is the love John shared for the place he calls home.

"Home means leaving, coming back, losing it, remembering, and having had one once, so we know it is neither magic nor beyond the horizon of possible imaginings. And sometimes home means you are loved and accepted and forgiven."

Ralph H. Blum, *The Book of Runes*

*N*eatly tucked away in the West End of Richmond amid a suburban landscape of orderly, expensive colonials, SUVs driven by small, trim women, and clusters of upscale strip malls anchored by a Starbucks or a Chipotle is the Virginia Home for Boys and Girls. It has been working for over a century to give a small group of children the chance to make up the definition of home for themselves.

The home was founded as the Male Orphan Society in 1846 by the Female Human Asylum after a boy came begging at their door asking for pennies. Later the name was changed to Virginia Home for Boys, and in 2003, girls were added to the title.

What can be called a home and who gets to define the terms is at

The entrance to the Virginia Home for Boys and Girls.

the heart of the controversy over the continued use of orphanages that is gathering steam in America. It's not an easy definition because with each politician, social worker, or children's advocate comes their own memories of home and hearth that they hold dear, their own sense of what's right, their own definition. And lately, everyone has been holding fast to their ideal version of family.

Opinions became particularly inflamed in 1994 after Newt Gingrich proposed removing unwed teenage mothers from welfare and placing their children in orphanages. It was a proposal by Gingrich to cut costs by breaking up families. Children's homes took the brunt of the backlash over the Dickensian proposal. The uproar was deafening.

I ran the idea of the book by the person I trusted most in the world, my father. Dad had been there almost from the moment I began my life as a writer. I had waited, too afraid I'd fail, until I was almost thirty and a single parent living in his new house with him.

It was those early assignments that started my habit of running each new project by Dad, telling him who I was about to go see or what adventure I was setting out on. Each time I was heading out to interview someone in my father's hometown, he'd pull out a memory to share.

"She has a hole in the side of her head," he said, about an elderly woman he had known as a teenager. I spent the interview trying to keep my focus on what she was saying. Fortunately, she pointed out the dent on her own.

Sometimes his odd recollection of background came in handy. He always seemed to know someone's true motivations and armed me with a perspective that made it easier to get them to open up.

"What do you think about a book on modern US orphanages? Tell all their stories?"

"Reminds me of the seminary," he answered. "All of the people there." He tried to tell me a story but choked up, tears easily pouring down his cheeks.

"You okay?" I asked, not used to seeing him cry so openly.

"I just love that place," he said. I didn't see the connection at the time between what I was asking and his answer, but that would come.

I chalked it up to a rare sentimental moment and set out to find out more about what makes up a home these days. Knowing I had him as a sounding board gave me confidence.

The first stop was the Virginia Home.

The home spreads out over thirty-five acres, lovingly tended, hidden behind the old West Tower movie theater, which is rumored to be slated for demolition and made into something else, maybe another grocery store. The easiest way to get to the home is through the parking lot of the old theater and down the back road by a parking lot dotted with tall weeds and blocked by a sagging chain across the entrance.

Take the small curve around the road to the back and abruptly everything changes.

The contrast between what has been neglected and the neat green lawns and swept paths of the home hidden away behind a busy main thoroughfare gives the whole place a sense of a secret garden, cherished by its inhabitants.

Using the word home, or orphanage, or institution are all dangerous words these days that instantly bring up strong emotions from people both inside and out. But which emotions will be sparked are tricky to predict. It's my first clue to tread softly with the inhabitants.

Collected in the home is an odd version of family—teaching parents, assigned *uncles* and *aunts*, and some forty-eight brothers and sisters—and just like any other family they all have different impressions of the place that they fiercely believe are true. But unlike the politicians or advocates, their feelings are based on a very personal reality, not the culling of arguments about "best interests."

Each year there's an open house for the public to come and see what goes on at the home, but the only takers are the regular donors and the homeowners from the nearby neighborhood who want to reassure themselves annually that there's nothing going on that might threaten their property values.

So far, there have been no cries of "not in my backyard" and the Virginia Home and their neighbors have co-existed quietly, side by side. There are six residential cottages, long low one-story ranch house-style structures, called ranchers in the south, painted tan and white, four for boys and two for girls, with the second one for girls just opened, and one independent living cottage for kids who age out and are legally adults but have no family to return home to. Girls have only been admitted since 2003 after administrators noticed how many girls were piling up in the separate emergency shelter the home operates.

The minimum age any child can be accepted into a residential facility in Virginia is eleven and the oldest is seventeen. Once they're in, though, they can stay till nineteen or twenty and everyone's sure they can get up on their feet. No one gets booted out the door on any certain

Residential homes at the Virginia Home for Boys and Girls.

birthday with a suit and a hundred bucks. There's an entire system in place called Independent Living to help each child who isn't going on to college, or has no family, make the transition to life in the community. Some have even been known to come back after college for a short stay. After all, it's their home, an alumnus pointed out without any irony.

The administration sits in a matching tan and white building, the last on the road toward busy Broad Street. A copper trimmed display case to the right of the entrance had a peg board last summer with the name of an alumnus, Marshall Thompson, winner of the Leadership Award from Virginia Commonwealth University, one of the local universities.

Near the administration building is the old dining hall, with long rectangular windows, yellowed with age, stretching down either side of the building, now used only at lunchtime by the campus school or by the home community during special occasions. Only six years ago all of the children at the home ate dinner together every night in that hall. Now

The new John G. Wood school.

they dine with their individual cottage "families," shopping and planning menus as a small group. There are some mixed feelings about which is better, with some of the alumni opposing any changes.

Further on down the gently curving road with neat rounded curbs is the small chapel where the new executive director, Chris Schultz, a young handsome man with perpetually tussled blonde hair and untested ideals, was recently married. Right now there's no chaplain or regular services of any kind, but the administration is thinking about it.

It might be nice to have someone around that the children can chat with and a place for faith to grow, muses Tod Balsbaugh, who has been a part of the place for over thirty-five years, first as executive director and now as director of development.

"But you have to be careful," he says, and not for the first time. "You can't be seen as pushing religion," he says. In the lives of children almost everything is guided by the individual state and the current politics. Pages and pages of state regulations guide their lives, more than is required for foster care or families waiting to adopt and, as in everything, there are both good and bad sides to that. Everything must be documented, and if there is one omission, like an aspirin given but not written down, the repercussions can be outsized to the offense. If caught during a twice-annual inspection by the Virginia Department of Social Services, the home would receive a citation, sometimes referred to as a "violation."

However, the chances for abuse to go unnoticed are smaller and the chances for a child to slip further into anger or depression are slimmer in the home than in foster care. Too many well-trained people have invested their time and effort in the child's success, working very hard to bring about a different conclusion.

"A child has to fall his way into this place," said Tod. "Have you heard that one before? Children who arrive here have usually been moved from pillar to post." Failed their way out of foster care is what he means. On average each child at the Virginia Home who has been placed through social services has been through five foster care placements in short order before arriving at the campus.

It's also his way of pointing out an obvious fact: that this place is more than "three hots and a cot," another old saying. It might seem silly that he was taking so much time to point out the obvious except for all of the drumbeats to close places like this. Well-meaning advocates see all of it as warehousing and want the facilities closed in a naïve hope that this will force the government's hand in fixing foster care. Naïve because since the mid-1980s the number of foster-care families has declined at the same time that children in need of their services has sharply increased and there's no sign that trend is changing. The government can't force people to become foster care families.

Tod knows about the prejudice that most of the visitors show up with. Influenced by what they've heard, they expect to see an institution that can only keep the children going until something better can be found. He shakes his head in exasperation and the words come out faster. "You end up feeling like it's necessary to show them some small problem so they'll finally relax and start to really see the place," he says, the first hint of cynicism creeping into his voice.

There's that idea again about who really gets to figure out whether or not a place is worthy of being called a home. It keeps coming up. But Tod in his heart is an optimist and he quickly returns to his favorite topic, the kids.

"I've seen miracles happen," he says. "A boy from Roanoke was adopted. The father was a doctor and the mother was a nurse. The family had three adopted children and then two of their own and eventually all of the adopted children were pushed out and left home. That happens, you know.

"The boy was placed here and he would call home and they would hang up the phone on him and refuse to see him at the holidays." His eyes dance around the room as he's once again imagining the boy who showed up on his doorstep, angry and abandoned not by just one family, but two.

"Hated his father, hated him. But I told him to never give up, keep the door open a crack. Keep that crack open. Then he went on to the army. Hadn't heard from him in a long time and he married a girl from Romania. I went to the wedding and guess what, the father was the best man. Could have knocked me over. Miracles happen, I've seen them. It'll spark." Tod is beaming. Another one of his children has found some peace, a little bit of happiness somewhere.

He has the same smile on his face for each child, a smile that looks hopeful and worrisome all at the same time as he yet again runs his hand through his salt and pepper hair. This is the part of parenting that makes the stomach flip and turn—wanting to protect a child from everything and knowing it's not possible and not even good for them. But you want it anyway.

Tod loves these children and takes them into his heart so deeply that he takes every phone call from anyone who has ever lived there and does whatever he can to help. It doesn't occur to him that it's not part of his job description anymore except in hindsight and even then only for a moment.

"I suppose I shouldn't..." is all he says, before another story, another child's success in spite of a childhood filled with abuse or neglect is being painted and the smile grows on his face. Every visitor is only the newest audience giving him a chance to show off all of his children. Someone worked out the math on how many children had passed through the home since Tod first arrived and the number turned out to be a thousand. Tod is an anchor for all of those children.

He was a young married man when he showed up at the home in January 1971 with his wife, Betsy, who passed away in 2002, and he had no idea he had stepped into the rest of his life. His previous brief career choice was as a Fuller Brush man and he quickly learned there wasn't enough fulfillment in it for him. He applied for the job of probation officer for Henrico County, the county the Virginia Home sits in, and was redirected to an opening at the home.

He ended up living on the campus, raising his family there, and letting each side become a part of the other. He only recently found a new home off campus.

Like any good family member would, he shows up at high school football games and graduations and now Chris Schultz does, too. Another anchor.

Tod sets another appointment to go out for a tour of the campus in two weeks time.

⧒⧓

And then everything changed.

My father died.

He was four states away with my mother, visiting my oldest sister, and had started to feel badly. That night he was dead.

My steadfast mooring was gone. Along with him went my routine, my ideas of what might happen next, my confidence, and our sense of well-being. I waited a day and a half to tell Louie, not wanting to unravel his life just yet, but I couldn't put it off any longer.

"I need to talk to you." I was trying to get him to come home. I'd been trying for hours but he kept finding something else to do, someone to visit. Standard teenage fare for a seventeen-year-old.

"Why? I'm busy. I'll talk to you later," he said, half-bored. I could feel my throat tightening. I wanted to be able to get through this, say the words.

"It's about Granddaddy."

"What?" he said, agitated. "Can't it wait?"

"No."

"Why? Is he dead?'

For a moment I couldn't catch my breath, couldn't say a word. I wanted to say something else, lead into it, cushion the words; but I couldn't think of a thing.

"Yes." It was all I said. I could hear the sudden intake of breath and then he was softly crying.

"Louie? You okay? Come home."

"No, not Granddaddy. How? Why? I'll see you later," he choked out the words in a hurry and hung up. It was almost all he'd ever say about it to me. He didn't give me the chance to answer any of his questions.

It felt like lately I had made a habit of failing Louie, not coming up with the right words. Learning how to live without Granddaddy wasn't the only recent hurdle.

Beginning in the first grade, it had become obvious to me that Louie was having difficulty reading. To avoid labels being placed on my young son, I did what I thought was best: I started reading to Louie. Every book he came into contact with, whether for school or for fun, I read to him. To keep him entertained while I read, I created funny voices or made comments about the plot lines that I found particularly far-fetched.

By the beginning of Louie's ninth grade in school none of my help was working anymore. His grades were failing and at long last, I had to ask for help.

I sat in a nondescript room, at a set of long folding tables shaped into an L and ringed by plastic chairs, and asked officials at the school to please test Louie for any possible learning disabilities. I explained he only had trouble with reading.

It had taken me fifteen years to get to that meeting.

I explained carefully, and repeatedly, that I didn't expect them to find anything seriously wrong. I assured them that whatever accommodations Louie might need, if any, would be simple.

Through elementary and middle school, Louie had grown into a thoughtful, intelligent, articulate young man who up until then earned mostly Bs, but who had trouble comprehending the little he could read. No one else knew, and Louie and I rarely talked about it.

His reading difficulty was the only problem I saw, and I accepted that everything else was fine. I told myself that I was doing the right thing because Louie might feel badly about himself if he thought there was something wrong and because mainstream colleges wouldn't accept a kid with learning disabilities. Fortunately, time and high school had finally caught up with both of us.

Louie's workload in ninth grade became so large that I couldn't read everything to him, and Louie was becoming too independent to want me to. He was also starting to fail in more ways than I realized. I knew that I had to find help, which led me to my request for testing and my pronouncement that Louie was in need of only a little help. But I still hadn't allowed myself to look at the depth of his disabilities.

John Ribble, a soft-spoken gentle man who was responsible for testing most of the students in the Henrico County system, called me in for a meeting after only the first round of tests.

He held out Louie's answers and said that based on these first tests Louie had a more acute problem than I had indicated. He pointed to an answer on a timed test that required more speed as it went along. Toward the end of the test, Louie had indicated that May was a day of the week. He hadn't had enough time to puzzle over the words. Ribble looked at me, still surprised, and said, "No one ever misses that question."

He pulled out old standardized test scores for Louie going all the way back that showed wild inconsistencies. He said the tests and Louie's school record suggested my son was not only visually processing impaired, their old term, but that he likely had attention-deficit disorder, and was suffering. Ribble pointed out this possibility again and again, mostly because I denied it firmly every time he said it.

"I'd know if he was struggling that much," I protested. "I'd be able to tell."

But I hadn't. I had ignored the clues because I didn't want to see them. Besides not being able to read much, Louie had always been habitually disorganized, didn't absorb instructions that went on for very long, and was easily distracted by sound or movement. All were signs of ADD.

As it turned out, Louie had dysgraphia, a short-circuit between the brain and the pen, as well. He not only couldn't comprehend what he was reading without a lot of difficulty, he couldn't easily write what he wanted to say without using a computer. None of it meant he wasn't intelligent, which he was, but all of it meant he had a specific way he needed to take in information, to learn.

When I told Louie about the diagnosis, he didn't look hurt or confused. Instead, his face relaxed and he shouted, "You mean I'm not stupid?!" I was so taken aback that I started to cry. Louie said, still very relieved, "Were you worried, too?" I cried harder.

By denying the truth to myself and thus keeping it from Louie, I had left him with the only other plausible answer he could come up with as to why he always worked so much harder than his best friends, Andrew or Anthony, and didn't get the same grades.

Ribble had called me in early because he had sensed that I was part of the problem. For all the parents who battled with lawyers and school administrators to get their children the tools they believed were necessary to make progress—and there were thousands around the country—here was a public school system trying to do the right thing, trying to bring the parent out of denial.

To reinforce his findings in case I gave him trouble, Ribble had polled Louie's teachers and found out that Louie had recently stopped turning in most of his homework, which meant he was outright lying to me. He tapped the grade sheets with all the zeroes and said it again, "Louie is giving up." Finally, I stopped talking and began listening.

I sat through Louie's first IEP meeting—the beginning of the process to design the "Individualized Education Program" called for under federal law—in somewhat of a daze. Over the next few months, we mapped out a plan to address Louie's weaknesses and bolster his strengths. Some of the accommodations were: grammar would be graded separately on any test where it was a factor in the score; math tests could be taken and answered orally; Louie could request to take a test in a separate room, away from distracting noises or movement; and he would have a resource time in the middle of every school day to go over any academic snags. Most importantly at the time, the school offered to pay for Louie to become a member of Recording for the Blind & Dyslexic, an organization with more than 90,000 CDs and books on tape in its library. The initial fee then was $75, and for $35 a year Louie could use the service for life.

Perhaps the hardest thing I did, though, was to take a long look at my own behavior. I had fallen into the trap of trying to make Louie conform to my own definitions of learning, instead of being open to the idea that he would have his own path. I thought I was protecting him by keeping the truth from him. Instead, Louie knew something was wrong, and I had left him alone to come up with his own answers.

I thought about all the years I hadn't helped Louie to look clearly at himself and celebrate who he really is, and I knew that had to change immediately.

To inspire Louie's natural artistic talent, (which is common among a lot of kids with dyslexia, though no one can say exactly why), I arranged for us to take a tour of the new arts building at Virginia Commonwealth University, my alma mater. Our guide was the retiring head of the department, Myron Helfgott. I told Professor Helfgott about Louie's learning disabilities before we got there.

During the tour, Helfgott made a point of telling us of a talented recent graduate who had such severe dysgraphia that he couldn't write at all, but had found his way nonetheless and thrived.

I had been wrong—there were mainstream colleges that take students with even severe learning disabilities, as long as the students know what accommodations they'll need and prove they can keep up. In other words, keeping Louie from learning about himself and getting help would have been the biggest factor in keeping him out of college.

Another thing I learned happened the first time a teacher tried to send Louie out of her room for being too distracted. I pointed out to the teacher and the principal that Louie was now protected under the federal Individuals with Disabilities Education Act or IDEA law, because he had an Individual Education Program or IEP and couldn't be punished for behavior related to his disability. Before, when I was staying so silent, Louie was still open to being labeled, but with worse labels. Now, he had protection. Most teachers learned right along with us what ADD meant and worked with us, and for the occasional one who didn't, the law protected Louie and kept him in the room to learn, bolstering his confidence in himself. He wasn't broken, just different, and it was okay.

When Louie got his first report card of his sophomore year I tried to look both congratulatory and empathetic as I waited for him to tell me how he had done. I didn't want him to think I didn't expect much or that I wouldn't be happy with whatever he had achieved. A tricky balance.

Louie had made the honor roll. A wave of relief came over me. Louie had stapled his report card down the middle to keep it open, and it already looked a little ragged.

"You've been carrying it around?" I asked.

"Yeah," he said, trying to sound casual.

"How about if I frame it?" I said, trying to do the same.

"Yeah," Louie said. "That'd be good."

It hung on the wall in his room that was situated across the hall from where Granddaddy, until that week, had lived. And now, instead of having years to get used to who he was and celebrating that, Louie had only had a few rocky years of us trying to figure out what he needed or even wanted to use as accommodations in school. I remember these years as ones in which I spent way too much time still holding up a bar and seeing if Louie would meet it. He knew it too.

Dad was the one who could let go of any invisible standards or fears about what a score on a test really meant and just laugh with Louie, letting him know there was a safe place for him.

And now he was gone, and Louie and I were left with just each other. My mother moved in with one of my sisters.

※

I kept the appointment with Tod, days later, and followed him around the campus, looking at each building, asking questions, focusing on the story. Tod pointed out features while relating them to some piece of Richmond history. "I'm not exactly sure when that happened," he said, as we came up the steps from the weight room.

The words were almost out of my mouth. "I'll check with Dad. I'll bet he'd know," when I remembered there was no one to ask and for once, I was on my own. It felt like the wind had been knocked out of me. I let the moment pass and didn't tell him.

"Did you see the sign out front?" Tod asks. "That's Marshall Thompson, great kid. He's going on to get his PhD. Another success story."

We came to a neat tan and white building halfway between the two

Home number thirteen—the Kelly home.

entrances, cottage number 12, occupied by Della and Chris Hill, the teaching parents. They're a young couple—Della is twenty-seven and Chris is just thirty—and they have already been foster parents and worked as teaching parents.

It's the middle of the day and all of the children are in school leaving only Della and Chris and their youngest son, four-year-old Mark at home. Their older son, seven-year-old CJ, is at public school. They're transplants from another home, the Utah Youth Village, where the same style of working with children was used, the Teaching Family Model, which has only been in place for six years—the reason for no longer having communal dinners on campus.

Della opens the door. She's tall with long straight brown hair, an earnest smile, and determined handshake and represents all the ambition in the family, returning to college for a master's and dreams of a PhD. Chris is more easy-going and the reminder to have some fun along the way. They easily finish each other's sentences and laugh at each other's jokes.

The immediate entrance is decorated by the home according to a standard established by the Virginia Home. There are neatly framed drawings of wild animals, a lion and a giraffe, a working fireplace, side tables with lamps, and a few assorted tchotchkes.

A comfortable couch, love seat, and chairs face away from the fireplace and directly at the over-sized television screen. Down the hall from the private apartment where the Hills sleep with their children and dog, Toby, a bouncy Boston terrier, and where the other children never venture, lumbers Mark in his pajamas with a Spiderman mask firmly in place. He saunters up, leaning over the arm of the couch, and lifts up the small rubber ball in his hand that looks like the earth.

"This is my world," he says slowly, his words bouncing off the inside of the mask, "and you live in it."

He wanders over to see his father, resting against him as he pulls the mask up to show his face. There's an impish grin as he tosses his world in the air. He's at home.

Before they worked as teaching parents at a home, they had two foster children and Chris worked as a manager at a restaurant, Della as a nurse. Neither one of them felt they were doing enough, giving something back.

Chris spotted an ad in the newspaper for the Utah Youth Ranch and they answered the calling. However, to fit into the state guidelines they had to let go of the two foster boys who they had grown to love. That was the tough part, but the state wouldn't allow the children to accompany them.

What drew them to Richmond was the Virginia Home's offer of tuition reimbursement, making Della's dream of a PhD possible.

The couple in the cottage next door both have master's and a new couple moving in to a nearby cottage are working on advanced degrees.

Each couple at the home must be married and thoroughly trained in the Teaching Family Model that is used in forty homes across North America and Canada and is spreading. The simple version is that it's a system of points given for good behavior such as greeting a visitor immediately with your name and a handshake, treating each other with kindness, keeping a neat room, or doing assigned chores like the dishes. Points can be earned even when the child isn't aware if one of the parents notices the good behavior, and they can be taken away as a consequence for negative behavior like fighting or the more common problem, a messy room. Enough points can mean extra privileges like weekend movies.

Recently one of the boys staying in cottage 12 put the point system to the test. Little Pete,* a seventh grader, was angry in general and trying to prove he was unlovable. He chose to play it out after his new roommate didn't keep their bathroom as sparkly clean as he felt was necessary.

Little Pete, as he's known to distinguish him from Big Pete, had complained loud and long about the unfair burden he was carrying at having such a sloppy roommate. But nothing was getting resolved to his satisfaction, so he decided to show the Hills a thing or two with a Boston cream pie and some baby powder.

He took his revenge out on the guest bathroom off the foyer while everyone else was watching television in the main room that adjoins the foyer, knowing full well everyone would see him walking back and forth. He made a trip to the freezer, took out the pie, and disappeared back into the bathroom.

Back and forth, back and forth, he went between the bedroom and the kitchen, daring anyone to stop him. The Hills watched him surreptitiously but didn't make a move to stop him.

"No power plays," explained Chris.

Finally, he wore himself out.

Chris went and took a look at Little Pete's performance art.

Baby powder was sprayed everywhere, coating the walls and floor,

---

*All of the children's names at the Virginia Home have been changed.

and he had tried to flush the frozen Boston cream pie down the toilet, clogging the whole thing.

Both of the Hills are laughing as they tell the ending.

Little Pete had to make restitution for the bathroom, which meant cleaning it up, and the roommate was switched to another room. I've heard worse just hanging around the parents in my own cul de sac. It's not only normal adolescent behavior, it's pretty tame and was a message that the Hills were able to decode.

Chris has seen worse. At his previous home he was bitten, scratched, had pipes thrown at him, and he has been called plenty of names. But these are kids who know no kind of permanence and by the time they reach the Hills, they have been lied to, abused, and abandoned. The anger has to get out somehow.

Good parenting is all about instilling in a child the belief that no matter what happens in the life ahead of him, he'll figure it out. That's it, and that's a tough job that requires stability, love and patience in large measures. It's even tougher when a child has had all of that stripped away from him, often more than once.

Chris and Della are calm and steady telling the stories of all of the children's lives they've influenced. More anchors who wait patiently for the child to see that a lot may be up for grabs but the Hills believe in them and are determined to teach them the same.

They arrived at the Virginia Home six months ago, which is the usual length of time, make-or-break, when a couple hangs in there or burns out. But they've been at this a total of four years and love what they're doing.

To ensure that most teaching parents don't burn out the Virginia Home gives each couple eight days off a month while a permanent alternate teaching parent comes in to the home and stays with the kids. There is also a mandatory two weeks of paid vacation with a $500 stipend.

"Virginia Home for Boys & Girls is making it so we can stay forever," said Chris.

Two residents playing football outside the Independent Living Home.

"My favorite parts of the day are when the kids start coming home," he said. "I get paid to help these kids. I get paid to play basketball, go to movies, let them vent about a girlfriend.

"I don't work here. This is my home."

They invite me back for dinner with all of the boys so I can get a chance to see everyone together and experience their home life.

A gaggle of boys of all sizes greets me at the door, all with hands outstretched waiting patiently for me to introduce myself and shake each hand in turn. No grunts or ducked heads like I'm used to with my own son and his set of teenage friends. It's almost refreshing. They're using what they've learned and earning points.

Chris is standing behind them, smiling proudly. "That's part of the Teaching Model," he explains as the boys wander back to the couches or keep a short distance behind me.

"I want to pick my own name. Call me Sinbad," says the tall, muscular teenager with dark brown skin and a smile that implies mischief. He had heard about the need for new first names.

Sinbad is one of the oldest in the house, a senior at Freeman High School, a nearby public school, and a varsity football player. He has seen a lot of different homes, most of them foster care, and came to the Virginia Home with 80 extra pounds, topping out at 285 on his six-foot frame, which he has worked at losing.

He has a half-brother and a twin at the home as well, all in separate cottages. The children used to live with their grandmother in the housing projects. One afternoon a car sped by strafing the building in an attempt to shoot down a rival outside. Sinbad's grandmother screamed for them all to get down, throwing herself on top of Sinbad. He survived while she took a bullet and died.

They became nomads after that, traveling from one address to another, unpacking their things, building up a little bit of a life before someone made a decision and the whole process started over again.

All of that hides behind the wide grin and stream of jokes.

"Hi, I'm Peter." It's big Pete, tall and blonde. He looks me directly in the eye before ducking his chin down, just like my son, Louie. Little Pete is right behind him and he shakes my hand eagerly, chattering away about what he learned in social studies the past week. "Do you know how Hitler died?" Apparently they're studying World War II.

Before I can give Little Pete an answer another hand is there from Malik, a Sudanese boy who survived the last civil war in his country and has come to America to live. There are a few Lost Boys from the Sudan at the home right now, their stay completely underwritten by the home, not anyone's government.

He speaks softly and I have to lean in to understand him.

Last comes Brian, small like Little Pete, who shakes my hand and asks me if I'd like to see his room, have I met the dog, do I have any kids.

"I'd love to, I have met the dog, and I have one teenage son, Louie. Give me a minute and then we can go take a look."

"Okay," he says anxiously and sticks by my side as we head for the kitchen. I can already smell the roast.

"Have you seen Chris's new toy? I got it for him as a surprise," said Della.

On the counter is a Ronco spit grill with a roast slowly turning. Big Pete heads for the kitchen and starts setting the table. Sinbad is playfully teasing Malik about his accent and little Pete is trying to tell whoever will listen about somebody else's demise in World War II.

A prospective teaching couple is there from Kansas to take a look around, and they're also staying for dinner. Brian and I take a quick shortcut to his room that he shares with Little Pete. There are two single beds pushed against opposite walls with matching thin burnt orange bedspreads, a dresser for each boy and homemade art work taped up everywhere. It's a boy's room, neat but only to a point, with lots of signs of life. Brian proudly shows off all of his portraits of Selena, the late-Tejano singing star. His walls are filled with them.

"She's my favorite. I really like her," he says. "I drew this one from this picture of her," he says, pulling out a picture from a folder overflowing with different photos of the singer.

"I don't really like it here," he mumbles, as he pulls out another picture of his idol.

"How come?"

"Too many rules," he answers, not looking up. "I can't wear really tight jeans and I can't grow my hair long." His hair looks like it's holding onto a little too much gel. Behind him on his dresser are neat rows of grooming products, enough for a salon.

"I liked it better at home. I could do whatever I wanted to there."

He changes the subject and talks about what life was like before he came to cottage number 12. It's a long story about the drugs he watched his mother, and a host of other people who came through the house, use on a regular basis. His definition of anything he wants to do has no boundaries.

Brian has gone back to a blank look that gives away nothing on the surface. It's only the speed of his words and the topics he chooses that give anything away. He ends the story with a quiet recitation of every illicit drug he can think of and their proper dosage. Like he's passing on the necessary information. Maybe it's still too much for him to believe in adults staying clean or sober, but if he stays vigilant, they'll at least live.

He is the one I have most wanted to put my arm around and tell him it'll be okay. But I know that's not what he needs. It's not what any of them need. They need to know healthy boundaries that stick because someone loves and cares for them. Otherwise, when they're grown they'll have no clue how to set them for themselves. My desire to make it all better by giving in, I mean after all it's a pair of jeans and some hair, is a bad idea. A bad road to start down.

Instead, I tell him that my own son can't grow his hair either and would love to.

"Really?" asks Brian, looking more than a little surprised. It doesn't seem to have occurred to him that rules can exist in families out in the suburbs, in the houses just beyond the borders of the home. It is as if I have just pulled back a piece of the curtain on the tired, old wizard.

"Yeah, we have rules. When he's grown he can make those decisions for himself, but until then I want him to try it out my way." I leave out that lately he's mostly been angry about everything.

"Why?" he asks, but before I can answer, Chris is at the door announcing dinner.

We pass by Sinbad's room where the walls are covered with his artwork and a drum set, paid for by a donor, fills up his side of the room.

Dinner is buffet style and the boys grab a plate and get in line. Paul, a tall redhead, fills a drinking glass to the brim with canned peaches, Sinbad takes an abundance of rolls, and Big Pete has a stack of meat. It is amazingly normal.

I notice my plate is a little sticky and ignore it, moving on, taking a seat between Big Pete and Sinbad.

"Did you know that Mussolini was hung up by his feet?" Little Pete asks excitedly from across the table. "He was the Italian dictator." I love this age. Information pours into them like a weird sponge and they toss back out whatever caught their fancy like they were one of the lucky few to learn it and they just want to share. It doesn't take long to realize it's mostly the gory stuff that has stuck with him. I'm not surprised. My son still takes offense when I beg off the details from some horror movie. His crowd loves those movies and the only details they give out are about the various ways the zombies died, not any plot twists.

"You really like all the gross parts, don't you?"

"Uh, huh," he says with such an open face and is off, telling me some other detail about how Hitler died. Amazingly, a few facts seem to have gotten inside and he offers those up as well, if only to set the scene for Hitler's demise.

"When do you learn about World War I?" he asks. He's worried that all of the shuffling around, from pillar to post Tod would say, has made him miss some other war and all of those fun, gross facts. Big Pete tells him that in high school they dish it out all over again with even more information.

"Oh, good," he says, again with that open face, letting out a sigh as he takes a bite of his dinner. He mentions the different places he's lived and says he's going to be going home by the summer. Maybe the new school will go over the wars he's missed, he mumbles mostly to himself.

I don't ask anyone if it's true that he'll get to go home and let pass the question of what choice would be better for the boy.

The average stay for any child at the Virginia Home is eighteen months, at which time they're generally returned home, which is not always the best solution. The home is not allowed to say they're a permanent solution, another argument won by the advocates for foster care. It means any child coming there keeps a feeling of instability even if the stay turns out to be a long, happy one, which also happens.

Dinner moves on and the small bits of stability they've found here dip back and forth with the horror they've known. The details are all meshed together and define normal for them. The conversation dances back and forth between the mundane, the hard, and the ridiculous. Big Pete is talking about the future.

"And what do you want to do after you graduate?"

"I'm joining the Marines," he says with the kind of pride that can only come from following in someone's footsteps.

"Your dad a Marine?"

"My dad's dead," he says, turning his face away briefly before adding, "Yeah, he was a Marine, in Vietnam." I wondered how it could be true. The war ended over thirty years ago when I was around Big Pete's age.

I change the subject, more for reasons of my own. We start firing factoids at Little Pete about World War II. He eats it up. Turns out Big Pete is a fan of Rommel's desert strategies.

There's something about all of this; it's a family held together at first by rules and then, as each child figures out how to trust the ground underneath them, by love and hope. Hope more about what they've found than anything, but it's something to build onto. Without that feeling that there are people in our lives who are steadfast everyone feels adrift and it makes it hard to take chances and step out into the unknown that life requires on a pretty regular basis.

These children need people who will stay long enough to work through the hurt and anger till they can find their footing. That's what each of these cottages holds and what many advocates of foster care with good intentions would like to take away.

As I leave, the boys are watching the latest Scooby Doo movie and Brian is hitting Little Pete with a pillow till Little Pete says he's had enough, a hard line that anyone must follow or risk losing a lot of points. Brian puts the pillow down. Sinbad is the most absorbed in the movie. After a quick vote on what to do that night, it's Friday and the chance for a treat, they're going to head out to bowling. Chris is sitting amongst the boys as I leave, smiling, and watching Scooby Doo with his arm around Little Pete.

Weeks later, Tod produces Marshall Thompson to talk about growing up at the home, knowing full well Marshall will not be what's expected.

He's twenty-three, has a gentle face and demeanor, tall and wearing jeans and a soft collared shirt. He blends right into the suburbs and looks like he was born and bred there. The truth is he's never lived any-where near a suburb. Preconceived notions quickly unravel as he tells the details of his life in a perfunctory manner.

He's the only boy in the family between two sisters, the older a half-sister, the younger a full sister, and he shared a household with his mother, Jeanne (pronounced Genie) and maternal grandmother, Helen, the matriarch of the family. Jeanne used to take him along on her illicit drug buys sitting him down in front of a television in another room when he was small and expecting him to entertain himself or sleep when he was older. She would be holed up in the bathroom all night with her new best friends doing coke and later heroin. Apparently Helen never tried to stop her daughter.

"I took care of the drug overdoses. Heroin, pain killers, Xanax, crack, valium." No flicker of emotion passes across his face. "I missed a lot of school growing up.

"My mother says when I was pretty young I would read to myself and I would sing to myself and put myself to sleep."

He says all of it matter-of-factly. The only signs of strain are when his breathing quickens or he taps hard on the notebook reminding me to get it right. But even then I'm sure he's not aware of it. His expres-sion is absent of emotion. He seems to be trying to say it was all no big deal.

He has one memory of his father who ran out on them. It was when he was six and his mother took him over to his father's house with his younger sister. He remembers playing with the man's dog and his father saying goodbye and handing him a two-liter bottle of change. That was the extent of it.

"My mother said he was a psychotic," he adds.

"How do you feel about your mother saying that about your dad?"

Marshall shrugs his shoulders and says nothing. The conversation moves on, it was a non-event in his mind, especially when compared with what was going on at home.

The sleeping arrangements in first a subsidized apartment building inhabited by single mothers, and then a cheap apartment nearby, were: each girl with a room to herself, Helen in another, and Marshall and his mother in the last bedroom, sharing a bed. He quietly says that nothing ever happened and we keep going. It's not my place to poke at anything too sharply or make demands of his story. All of this is his to tell. He's at least earned that and I can't heal any of this just by listening.

Helen was never particularly kind to Marshall either. There were unexplained marks on Marshall's back as a child that Helen would explain away as necessary because the boy had done something wrong. She was forever telling Marshall not to cry. Showing emotion was a sign of weakness, she said.

"My mother said I reminded Helen of her dead son who killed himself," said Marshall.

"I don't know if that was nice of her to say or not," he says. We never stay too long on the negative aspects of Jeanne.

No matter what their home life may have been, when the two of them were out together, Helen maintained an illusion that everything was fine. She would quote Shakespeare and take him to movies at the Westhampton Theater or to the local symphony. There were two separate parts to Marshall's life that didn't cross over into each other—the drugs and violence versus the outings, particularly to the movies. They went to a lot of movies.

He still loves to relate anything in his life to a movie.

"I could give you a hundred different movies and a hundred different scenes and tell you how it all fits my life." He's finally smiling, suddenly sitting back in his chair. We pick out different movie scenes that we either loved or hated. The conversation meanders away from the old nightmares for a while but Marshall unexpectedly takes it back there.

"My mother was really fat, three hundred pounds, and didn't bathe for years at a time," he said.

"Really?" I ask, a little caught off-guard.

"Yeah, but you can get used to my mother's smell," he says, as if he's apologizing for Jeanne. He lets out another story, explaining the many sides of his mother.

"I was in the Center of Humanities and I had a really expensive laptop that I had checked out from the Center that my mother had beaten with a baseball bat and I was afraid to go back to school," so for a while he didn't. Teachers called once in awhile wondering where he was, but it wasn't until someone explained to his mother that she'd lose her benefits that she made him go back.

"She wasn't all bad, though. I saw the movie *Space Camp* and loved it. Did you see it? I really wanted to go to space camp, just like the movie. My mother wrote three hundred letters to different corporations, did all of the investigative work herself, got a free plane ride, and spacesuit. Rockwell International paid for the airfare and different corporations were sending me things. That was all my mother," he said, tapping my notebook hard.

But Jeanne was also the one who called social services when Marshall was ten and said they'd better come and get him or she'll kill him.

"Why they took me and not my sisters, I don't know," he said, "because if my mother was capable of killing me ..." he shrugs his shoulders again as if he's saying, it was something about him. Maybe he had failed.

He was placed in foster care but according to Marshall the family used the money they received from the state for his care to go on excursions to Atlantic City instead. They weren't particularly thrilled he was there. Eventually they called social services claiming he was a problem and Marshall was moved again.

He loved the second family. Some of the better memories from his childhood are wrapped up with them. But by now his mother was raising hell with the social worker and telling her son he was being mistreated. Marshall loved her and wanted to believe she cared about him. He went along with all of it.

A lot of older children don't want to be adopted, no matter the hell they came from. They wish for their old families to straighten up and fly right and they can't dream of what they've never seen, never experienced. A new family that operates out of love and concern is too hard to fathom.

Many believe it would only be a new hell without the blood ties. Best to dream of a better day with what is already known.

Marshall took his anger out on the new foster family, defending his mother.

"The word that comes up a lot was that I was an instigator," he said. Jeanne had control over him, even then.

"If I could find that family I would apologize," he almost whispers. He was removed from the family.

What was deplorable two years ago was suddenly acceptable to the system that had briefly tried to rescue him. He was sent back home where nothing had changed.

Up until the moment he landed in that second foster family, Marshall had thought his existence was not only normal but average. All of the drugs, the violence, the scenes of paramedics jamming a needle into his stepfather's chest, and the quiet burning anger of his grandmother about her lot in life were all a normal part of growing up.

But now he knew better and some small hard piece, a belief, deep inside Marshall wanted more. He wasn't going down with all of this mess.

He picked up the phone and called the Virginia Home for Boys & Girls and asked for help. He'd heard a social worker mention the place and he reached out to save himself. He was twelve years old when his life finally changed and started to take shape.

"I've learned all the day-to-day things I know from an institution," he says. He learned how to set a table, make a bed, bringing the illusion of his grandmother, Helen's perfection, a little closer to the reality. He didn't act out this time, as much from hitting bottom emotionally as not wanting to be sent back home again.

"After living with my mother and living in foster care I did not need another family. I was more sad, depressed, miserable, quiet, shy. I was so worn down I just didn't care anymore."

It took him time to relax and trust what he had found. It's like Chris Hill said, some kids act out immediately. They are the easier ones to deal with. For others a year goes by and they're still uncomfortable. They're the tricky ones because it can be impossible to predict when the breakthrough will occur and how large the moment's going to be. Marshall was one of the latter.

The moment of acceptance came in an unusual form years after he had arrived at the home. It was a merging of the two sides of Marshall. For the first few years he hid the truth about where he lived and what his home life had been like from all of the new friends he made at school. But it got harder to explain things away. "I started to get to the age where people want to call you or give you a ride home."

Marshall worried that if his friends knew the truth about his living situation they'd think less of him; a common issue among the children. Being at a home, or in foster care, or in anything but the family you started out with can be seen as a stigma. Other people wonder what the child did to end up there. It's a judgment of a person's worth. The child knows it and works at keeping the home a secret, worried there's something inherently wrong with him. that the truth about where he lives will be revealed.

For a while Marshall worked at silence, until once again he reached out and saved himself. He agreed to have his life portrayed, warts and all, in the *Richmond Times Dispatch*, the local paper.

"It was the most liberating thing," he says, letting out a deep sigh, "because I found out no one really cared. It was a relief I didn't have to live a lie anymore." Part of Helen's legacy was finally put to rest. He went on to William and Mary College in Williamsburg and then Virginia Commonwealth University for his master's.

Not all of Marshall's demons are gone. He still wonders if he has to earn respect and love. And if he doesn't work as hard, and keep earning honors, will he have as much of either. But there's time and lots of people around who love him to help him continue to shed outdated ways of thinking or coping.

Truth is, Marshall still loves both Jeanne and Helen and tends to their needs even now. Helen is in a retirement home, and his mother, who he says hasn't changed much over the years, is still living in an apartment. He defends both of them, saying they did the best they could and loved him the best they knew how.

Marshall makes the mental pockets for various pieces of his life in order to come to terms with who he is related to by blood, but his definition of who is family lies in the lovingly tended thirty-two acres just off a busy Richmond thoroughfare. His family is made up of the people who had a different kind of expectation for him than his grandmother: to be independent, to thrive, and, most, of all to be happy. He includes everyone who works there as his family and thinks of all of the children he grew up with as brothers and sisters.

Marshall is the one who laments the loudest that they've changed the basic system at the home from doing everything as a campus to a more home-like setting amongst the cottages. He thinks something has been lost, and maybe he's right, but what's more important is what Marshall is doing. He's defending his family and wishing they'd never change, just like anyone who has left the nest.

At a recent dinner sponsored by the Virginia Home for Boys & Girls Chris Schultz, as executive director, spoke about all of the great things the home was doing, referring to it repeatedly as a great institution.

Marshall was up next but before he started his speech wanted to clear something up, bristling a little as he started.

"First of all," he said, "this isn't an institution. This is my home."

⧼⧽

Only a few short months after visiting the Virginia home, a few short months after Dad died, the family sold the house to a woman who had shown up on our doorstep the day after Dad died, saying how sorry she was to hear of his passing, could she have a tour? I had refused, quietly shutting the door. But she persisted, contacting my siblings and the house was sold, for cash, in no time at all. The only home Louie remembered was sailing out from under us. Possessions were being catalogued and packed away and pieces of Granddaddy were disappearing quickly.

There was nothing I could do about any of it but tuck one of my father's handkerchiefs into my purse, give one to Louie, let go, and embrace the changes. They had a right to sell the house. It was never ours.

In the middle of it all there were moments of grace. At the funeral my only brother, Dabney, leaned over toward my son and asked him if he'd like to carry the box containing our father's ashes to the grave site. It was such a quiet act of love that recognized how important the connections were to a teenager. It allowed him a small moment of closure. Sometimes when I watch my brother, I can see traces of our father, not only in his movements but in his gestures that empower others without taking anything away from himself.

My mother stayed in Florida with my oldest sister, never really returning except for an occasional visit. I found a place to rent, my first place in fifteen years. Walking around inside the older townhouse I was close to tears and said to the very patient woman who worked there, "A start's a start."

"Yes," she said, emphatically, "a start's a start." She seemed to understand that the ground was shifting underneath me and I wasn't absolutely sure I was going to stand up and keep going.

Dad died in April, and we moved in the last few days of October on Louie's eighteenth birthday. We heard from no one. He sat on the stairs of our new home and asked me, "Why?" His voice full of anguish.

I had let go of them, they had let go of me, and with it, they had let go of Louie. I don't think any of us really knew what we were doing. There were no bad guys in this part of the story. Everyone was trying to do what they thought was right; trying to react and behave with kindness. Without Dad, though, I don't think any of us knew the language anymore.

Chapter 2

What's in a Name?

The story of Girard College, Philadelphia, Pennsylvania, founded in 1848 from a bequest in the 1831 last will and testament of Stephen Girard.

CHARLIE'S STORY

> "Courage is resistance to fear, mastery of fear, not absence of fear."
>
> **Mark Twain**

*T*he circumstances that led to Charlie Kalata, then seven, and his younger brother, John, becoming residents at Girard College are part of the ordinary grief that can bring families, if only temporarily, grinding to a halt as they deal with the unexpected consequences of a death in the family. Their father, Casimir, suddenly died in 1951 leaving their mother with some decisions to be made. Any death tears at the fabric of a life we've built, unraveling hopes and dreams, and requiring new plans which are drawn up at a quicker pace with the weight of so much loss mixed in with them. They were living in Wisconsin where the boys were born when Helen packed up her family and headed for home and Philadelphia.

Shortly after she moved in with two of her sisters someone told Helen about the Philadelphia institution. "They told her it was all free, a great education. We arrived here in April and by fall I was taking admissions tests," said Charlie. Not too long after that Charlie was a brand new second grader at Girard College wearing knickers and garters, part of the old costume, adjusting to more change in his young life. And in line with the policy of the time, his mother signed over custody of her children who became wards of the orphan court.

"I didn't mind the school, it was a nice place. Once you got here and they distract you by telling you to put away your clothes or go play with the other boys ..." His voice trailed off, lost in the memory.

When he turned around, his mother had gone home. The homesickness, he said, only lasted for a few days, mostly at night after the lights went out. Everything was regimented, helping the young boy adjust. "You marched into the shower, you marched out of the shower," he said, chuckling. "When you're seven if they tell you to line up, you line up."

And yet, given all of the loss and the change, Charlie and his brother adjusted and saw the possibilities in the new opportunity. "As a little kid I loved the Saturday afternoon movies. There were two types. Action adventure cowboy movies and action adventure with Russell Johnson in it," he said laughing. The actor, who was best known for playing the professor on Gilligan's Island, was a Girard graduate. "We saw every B picture he ever made.

"In a lot of ways it was wonderful, it was comfortable. My mother didn't abandon me; she showed up for mass on Sunday mornings and we stopped at the candy store on the way back." Students couldn't go home on the weekends until the fifth grade.

That policy, along with requiring parents to sign over custody, changed in later years and now all of the students who can, go home every weekend, for the holidays, and summers, and parents retain full custody. It is still a requirement that every child come from a single parent home at the time of admissions.

"It wasn't easy on my mother, but it gave her a leg up," said Charlie.

"She was a bookkeeper and she didn't have to work two jobs and we got extras we wouldn't have gotten."

And it enabled their family to continue what they would have had, if their father had lived. "I think that had my father lived we would have gone to college but in a different state and probably in agriculture.

"After he died, I'm sure I wouldn't have gone to college. I would have ended up in the trades. Not that there's anything wrong with that but Girard expected us to do well. After Girard, I didn't fit in my neighborhood anymore. It was just a different outlook on life. I wasn't ready to get married at 18 and have kids and go be a machinist."

Charlie graduated from Girard in 1962, started in construction in 1973, and attended Temple University in Philadelphia earning a BA in 1979. While he was still in college, he started a thirty-year career in construction as an estimator and project manager. He's been married to Vera for forty years, and their wedding day fell on the anniversary of his father's death, October 17, giving him something nice to think about on that day instead, he says.

They now have three daughters, Jennifer, Stephanie, and Katie. "There was never a question that my children would go to college and graduate and they all have." With the help of Girard College, Charlie and his family were able to get over the hurdles and pass along his late father's legacy to his daughters. In every family we can pass down the things we own from one generation to another, building wealth, but all of that can rot or be taken. It's the intrinsic values and the forging of a path ahead that can help a family tree take root, but sometimes a little help from a nurturing gardener is necessary to help the tree survive.

"It is one of the most beautiful compensations of life that no man can sincerely try to help another without helping himself."
Ralph Waldo Emerson

*I*t is a wall of sound. A swirl of tween girls moving everywhere, talking as they move quickly from one room to another. Pre-teen bodies in all shades of brown to pale white are twirling, singing, brushing hair, playing jacks, and talking, always talking. Chatter overlaps itself and twists around as a smaller girl in glasses, Andrea, breaks in on first one conversation and then another. No one misses a beat as the conversations lap over each other and she moves on with the rolling wave of sound.

It's a standard Sunday night in April, and all across the campus children from first grade to seniors, with an average stay of nine years, are returning from their weekend at home, in another life, to their dorm rooms at Girard College. The name "college" is a misnomer, given to the home by the founder, Stephen Girard to enhance the stature.

The entrance to Girard College.

Girard, who was the Bill Gates of his era, died in 1831 and left *the will* anyone with control issues would find comforting. Each bequeath was accompanied by very detailed instructions about the recipient as well as how the money was to be used. This reached its zenith with the details about the college. A small sampling of the details left behind about Founders Hall reads, "shall be constructed with the most durable materials, and in the most permanent manner, avoiding needless ornament and attending chiefly to the strength, convenience, and neatness of the whole.... There shall be in each story four rooms, each room not less than fifty feet square in the clear; the four rooms on each floor to occupy the whole space east and west on such floor or story, and the middle of the building north and south ..."

The children enter the grounds through impressive stone pillars, surrounded by walls that make a clear distinction between the Fairmont neighborhood outside and the campus inside, and pass by large marble buildings that would be at home on any ivy-league college campus. It was the effect Girard had intended—to raise the standards the children held for themselves beginning with their new environment.

Most of the children will be taking their school uniform—plaid skirt for girls or grey slacks for boys, white shirt, burgundy blazer and black shoes—out of their backpack or suitcase and getting their clothes ready for another Monday.

The seniors, who wear blue blazers to distinguish their position on campus, will come back wearing the jacket. They don't try to hide where they attend school and live during the week from those they leave behind in their neighborhood.

It's a symbol of maturity and learning to blend two distinctly different worlds: the bustling neighborhood and people they have momentarily left behind and the stately, manicured grounds and imposing buildings of Girard College that comes with a daily schedule and set of rules. They are learning to leave behind what they have known for an opportunity to change and become something new. It is one of the harder lessons in life and very few of us ever handle it without a few hiccups. In my age group they call it a mid-life crisis. But standing there amidst the girls, watching them say goodbye for the week to a loving parent who has opened up their definition of parenting and let go of so much control, and to the child who has stepped into the unknown based on a willingness to stretch beyond what they know, I know it's the same lesson all the way around. It's not one I have handled with much grace lately.

In the seventh grade dorm girls are catching up with each other and jostling for attention. Three residential advisors watch over the forty-four girls who range in age from twelve to fourteen years old in three separate living areas on the second floor of the Old Junior School building that sits across from the new running track and has the café, called the Hum, on the first floor. Everyone has been waiting for flavored Italian ices to go on sale at the café now that the weather is warmer.

All residential advisors, what other homes call house parents, live down the hall in furnished apartments and work three days on, one day off.

The idea of the close proximity to the living space is to provide a financial benefit to the RA, while giving the advisors some time off away from the constant activity. But the walls are thin and each advisor can hear the girls and knows when one of them needs attention. It can be hard to ignore.

That strong bond is created anew each year. It's still evident when August comes and last year's girls, now in eighth grade, come back and try to hang around. They have to be gently shooed away, to move on to the next step in their growth into responsible, independent young women.

They will only be together for this year; these three RAs constantly turning back the parenting clock to seventh grade with each new crop of children. "I prepare myself for it," said Quanda Robinson, thirty-seven, a native of Philly and an RA at Girard for the past six years. She has a kind face with soft, heavy lids and dark eyes that are easy to read. Always willing to listen and to assist, but she's not going to do it for you. Even with that in mind, there's a lot of commitment of time with this choice of career.

"There hasn't been a time when I've been off-duty that I haven't gotten a phone call or a knock on the door. Most people separate their work life from their home life but here it's impossible," she said.

It would be the same as having a babysitter at your house while you work in an upstairs office when suddenly one of your own cries out. It can take some willpower and letting go to turn over the reins, but it comes with the job.

"I still haven't gotten used to that," said Miss Robinson, as the children call her.

The children come knocking when they feel uncertain or are in need of someone to talk to, to the familiar face, often bypassing the substitute who fills in when Miss Robinson is off-duty. It can be hard to turn it off and work on a hobby or just watch TV. "It's really hard when you're sick and don't want to be bothered," she says with a sigh, followed quickly by a small laugh.

I know it has been one of my weaker areas as a parent. I stepped in too quickly to solve problems, help with homework, or mediate a dispute. I taught Louie to be afraid of failure. It came from my own fears that there might be no bottom, just an endless freefall. I was getting the chance to see my over-parenting reflected back at me in a new light from every direction.

I drove up here from Virginia, leaving eighteen-year-old Louie to fend for himself for two days and show up where he's supposed to, when he's supposed to. So far, though, phone calls to Louie while I've been on the road have been mostly ignored. When he does pick up it's to tell me to quit calling, stop bothering him.

I am getting an immersion course in good parenting skills as I watch RAs interact with the girls. But it all feels a little too late for me. It's a strange place to find myself in; seeing how to fix a relationship that's supposed to be almost done. All I can think is maybe there's something

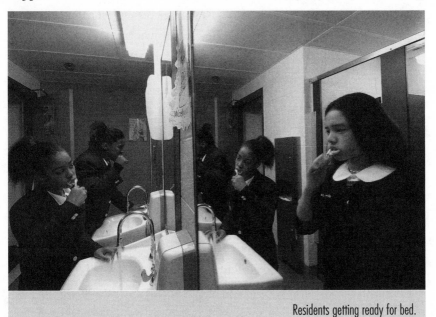

Residents getting ready for bed.

here for me to learn. Maybe there's a reason I'm here. I hold on to that thought to keep from drowning in my own parenting mistakes and try Louie again. It's 8:30 on a school night. No answer.

Miss Robinson reminds a couple of girls that it's almost time to be getting ready for bed. "I think you have to be built for this sort of thing," she says, watching over the girls.

It's a career shift for her, which is a little unusual at Girard. Most of the RAs come from the non-profit world. "I was in the hotel industry and I just wasn't happy there. And I got promoted three times in one year!" she said, still looking a little surprised at finding out money and prestige weren't going to cut it for her.

She moves among the girls easily, keeping an eye on them without hovering. Listening to complaints or requests or worries without becoming anxious, without jumping into the dramas.

Miss Robinson is still adjusting to the constant parenting that middle schoolers require, even when she's off duty. At least when it's your own kids you know they'll grow out of it. But at any residential education facility the adolescent phases are a constant; it's the faces that change, requiring patience for the new child who is experiencing hormone overload for the first time. For Miss Robinson it will be the sixth year, times 22 girls.

"There's one question I always get asked," said Miss Robinson. "'Do you have kids?' And I want to ask them, how many kids do you have in the seventh grade?" she says, reflecting on how hard it can still be for the parents to let go enough during the week, and to respect what Miss Robinson has to offer. "I think I'm an expert in seventh grade," she says.

Some of the mothers, particularly of the girls, have a tougher time with turning over so much parental control to another woman. It's a little too close to home. The boys' side sees less of the pop-up parent who drops by a lot unexpectedly to check on their child. The male resident advisors are seen as allies, there to fill in the male role model that may be missing. Overwhelmingly, the parents are single mothers.

Early the next morning, before seven a.m., Miss Robinson looks tired, sitting behind her desk in the large open common room, from where she can see the buzz of activity through the open doors of the four different bedrooms. Chores are getting taken care of, students are getting dressed, or looking for a lost book. A couple of girls are looking through homework.

"If I didn't have to get up early, this would be the perfect job," says Miss Robinson, smiling broadly, as an urgent voice tries to talk over her.

"Miss Robinson, Miss Robinson..." It's Joyce, a small thin girl standing in front of Miss Robinson's desk, repeating Miss Robinson's name until she gets her attention.

"What do you need?" Miss Robinson asks slowly in a low voice. Joyce spins out a story about the broken button on her white school shirt. Miss Robinson calmly asks her questions, each one directed at who was really responsible for the care of the button or the shirt. Joyce verbally comes at her from different angles, giving small, brief smiles before trying another line of argument to get someone to fix the shirt for her. None of it works. She smiles and goes back to getting ready for the day, promising to resolve the button issue on her own.

"I knew you could," says Miss Robinson. Joyce comes from a supportive family with an involved mother. She was just doing what most young teenagers like to do as sport. Arguing as conversation. It can wear a body out but Miss Robinson has moved on to the next request. Someone needs tape to finish their entry in the spring door contest.

"I didn't think they were doing it," she says, "but apparently they are. It's a secret." They're doing it in their rooms and are going to hang it up at the last minute. There is a lot of muffled whispering as the finished project is getting taped up.

Most of the girls in Miss Robinson's care are athletes, it's softball season, and art is not normally a favorite. But they've gotten together on their own, organizing who will do what, gathering the supplies and are now anxious to show it off. It's a nice picture of spring. The flowerpot has a 3-D quality, protruding out from the door.

Miss Robinson nods her approval. "Maybe we'll win this year."

The girls line up briefly for announcements before heading off to breakfast with one girl taking the lead, asking if there are any announcements, any birthdays. Before the recent renovations that created separate bedrooms and separate common areas with additional RAs on the same floor, Miss Robinson had twice as many moving bodies to keep track of. More regimentation was required. Now, she has found herself dialing back the commands and using a more fluid approach, teaching the girls about self-sufficiency, getting them ready for the eighth grade where there is a more hands-off approach.

Outside there are students in maroon and blue blazers moving in different directions between the buildings. Some of the kids have individualized the school uniform by rolling up pants legs, wearing large earrings, wearing small pins on the lapel or turning the coat inside out. A lot of that will get set right later in the day when they go on to school.

In the courtyard between the main buildings there are clusters of

The cafeteria at Girard College.

teenagers chatting before being broken up and moving on to classrooms or breakfast.

The middle school is filing into Banker Hall and up the middle staircase, depositing book bags along the way. Each meal is timed so that the number of kids eating together is limited, cutting down on chaos.

Meals are held cafeteria style on the first floor of Banker Hall with kids moving through a line and sitting at pre-designated tables with the RAs at a separate table. Kids having a particular issue on any given day can find themselves sitting with the adults.

The middle school boys are already in line getting sausage and eggs or cereal, pushing their trays along. One of the boys is wearing a Scooby Doo tie with his school uniform. Jason Davis and Kirby Lavell, two of their RAs, are nearby, coaxing the boys along and offering up wisdom about sixth and seventh grade boys.

"The boys never lose anything," says Mr. Lavell. "Everything was stolen. If they can't find their blazer, somebody stole it." Both of the young men are chuckling. "I like to ask them, 'Who do you think would want your school blazer?' Or if it's sneakers, 'Who has exactly your size and would want your sneakers?'"

Mr. Davis nods along with him, smiling and glancing over at the boys every now and then. "And later on they'll find it and then it's 'oh, I must have lost it.'"

The two men are trading another story as a small contest of wills is erupting behind them. Two boys are starting to trade insults quietly under their breath. Quickly, the argument has escalated to the bumping of chests. Mr. Davis and Mr. Lavell quietly and firmly step in and suddenly there are two more sitting at the RAs table, at opposite ends, occasionally giving meaningful glances to each other.

Everyone keeps eating their eggs, asking about the girls' roller skating outing planned for that night. After things have had a chance to cool down Mr. Kirby begins to indirectly address the situation, in between bites.

"This is how you can turn a day around," he says in a gentle but firm voice, his long braids gently bouncing against his shoulders. He is addressing the table in general, drawing in anyone who will listen. The boys have their chins down but both of them are looking at Mr. Davis, listening. He starts to look at each of them directly. "We can each learn how to communicate," he says, and keeps talking in the same even tone. Learn how to talk to each other and come to an understanding without violence or grudges.

Johanna Mudry, a twenty-six-year-old from nearby Phoenixville, and another RA for seventh grade girls has moved to the center of the room and is working at getting everyone's attention.

Dishes and silverware have been found in the trash again, despite repeated requests and direct orders to be careful. There is a brief lecture about unnecessary costs and where the money might have to come from—extras or treats—as she works to impress the need to be responsible. Actions followed by consequences, which bears no judgment of right or wrong, is a constant learning tool.

It's an antsy morning, though.

A boy, a smaller seventh grader, is standing by the food line quickly downing a juice glass full of an even mixture of syrup and orange juice. Another kid paid him two dollars. He finishes off the concoction and smiles.

Mr. Kirby shudders and calls him over. It's one of his. "You need to make better choices," he says, a little exasperated and grossed out at the same time. "No more sugar for you today." The boy is still smiling, holding on to his money.

When it comes time to leave, Mr. Kirby and Mr. Lavell release their charges but the girls are not paying any attention and get the opportunity to practice lining up quietly a few times. Eventually they get to leave, off to join the other students at the start of another day.

The entire student body goes home on the weekends and holidays, except for the occasional child whose family life has broken down to the point where other arrangements have to be made. That doesn't happen often, but when it does, Girard finds a way to create a campus family around the child. People who live on campus, like the president, and former alum, Dominic Cermele, who has been known to have an extra child or two at his table for Thanksgiving, become the weekend family.

The school was never a traditional orphanage, even though Stephen Girard referred to the first inhabitants as "poor male white orphans" in his will. They have always been children with a living parent, as were most of what we generally think of as orphans in America. Almost every child in latter-day orphanages has always been a 'social' orphan. They had at least one parent but needed a different place to grow up. A new chance.

In the past the head of household of Girard families was always a mother, but now the school is seeing a lot more children being taken care of by a grandmother or aunt. Occasionally, there is even a single father. None of the children are from social services.

Some of the parents use the opportunity of more time and less strain on the family budget to get ahead or go back to school. It's not unheard of for a Girard parent to work on self-improvement, even earn a degree while their child progresses from first grade to graduation. A new path is being built for more than one and a chance for success that spreads out further, touches more lives than just parent or child.

In 1960 the home dropped the word orphanage altogether and declared itself a boarding school with a few unique entrance requirements. Students still had to be white males who were citizens of the United States, from single parent homes, whose income was at the poverty level. The parent had to sign over complete custody of their child to Girard, while all tuition was paid for by the endowment of the school. In other words, the school endeavored to drop the stigma attached to the word home or orphanage, but changed little else. Potential residents were now called students and they had to apply, showing adequate grades with recommendations—mostly about behavior—from teachers and mentors.

Today, most applicants come from the surrounding Philadelphia area, which gets first consideration, and the children must still come from single parent homes and meet HUD economic guidelines. The children still live in dormitories and eat in a dining hall. Other, more traditional homes have changed to pattern themselves more closely after a family unit. Girard's style is now more like the elite boarding schools it emulates.

Founders Day, when all of the parents come to visit, used to be known as "No Daddy Day" with a dearth of male energy on campus for that day. It wasn't until the 1970s that the school stopped requiring the parent or guardian to sign over custody of their child to the school, as outlined in the last will and testament of Stephen Girard, and the parent can be mom or dad.

That phrase is used a lot by the administrators to explain why something is done the way it's done—it was in the will.

It's an ironic lesson about control and life in general at a school that requires so much change. Sometimes, a little letting go is going to be required and change will have to be let in the door. However, that control also became a model.

Milton Hershey, the chocolate king, visited Girard College before writing his will and used the school and the will as a template for his own designs that has become the billion dollar-endowed, better-known Hershey school in nearby Hershey, Pennsylvania.

A lot of people, including some at Girard, have asked why I wasn't visiting Hershey instead—the super-sized example of former orphanages that now has more of a resemblance to the most elite upper crust boarding schools. It's a testament of how well known Hershey has become, appearing on *60 Minutes* and in national magazines, that even some Girard administrators would wonder why anyone would bypass Hershey and head for its smaller cousin.

Hidden in Hershey's shadow, Girard College has a smaller endowment of only $500 million (still miles ahead of most other REFs), an operating budget of $22 million, and 720 students from K through 12, set on a leafy forty-three acres with a campus of buildings registered as historical landmarks.

Even though it's already been over 150 years since Girard's death, his presence is everywhere. In almost every room, and in different places *all over* campus, are busts, statues, drawings and paintings of Girard in various stages of his life. In Founders Hall there is an oversized painting, created for an episode of the CBS reality show *The Amazing Race*, that turned out so well the school asked if they could have it.

Elizabeth Laurent, associate director of historic resources, a fellow Virginian, oversees the vast collection of Girard memorabilia that includes pictures of groups of former students in early nineteenth century high collars, and piles of shoes waiting to be fixed at the now defunct campus cobbler manned by a professional. The children have always helped out with chores but were at Girard with the intent to get an education. In a large room in the back of Founders Hall are the personal possessions of Girard set out to dazzle students and visitors. Furniture is arranged exactly as he might have had it in his drawing rooms in Philadelphia and in nearby glass cases sits an impressive display of silver and china. Off to the side is an elegant coach in need of a set of horses. There are also the expected portraits of the man as well.

Every decade of Gerard's adult life is represented repeatedly on campus—merchant, mariner, banker, farmer, humanitarian. The most predominant age, though, is when he was a senior with one bad eye, sunken back into the framework of his face. Some of the paintings are skillfully painted from a three-quarters angled view so that it's less obvious.

At the front of the high school building are three tall stained glass windows. The middle window is a nice array of Girard in all his roles: mariner, founder, farmer and humanitarian. The left window carries a Girard affirmation, "I would have them taught facts and things and the purest principles of morality." The right side is dedicated to fallen veterans.

More change was forced upon Girard College in 1968 when a successful challenge to the will integrated the school, and the first young African American men, four of them, were admitted to the school. The first to graduate, Charles Hicks in 1974, is now on the board of managers. Girls were admitted more quietly for the first time in 1984.

The school has in the past struggled with change and paid the consequences. Sometimes it's a small lesson like the layout of Founders Hall. What Girard didn't anticipate was hallways. To access the rooms toward the back, students had to pass through every other room. Other times it has been more profound, like the struggle over integration, which led to a famous speech given by Dr. Martin Luther King, Jr. outside the gates. An official marker now stands just outside the school commemorating the event.

The school has also changed its earlier policy toward the neighborhood, Fairmount, that surrounds them. "We're forming a relationship with the community around us," said Frances Smith, head of the School for Education. "We're opening our gates more. It used to be the philosophy to keep the parents out, keep the neighborhood out." They had a picnic to benefit victims of Hurricane Katrina and invited in the neighborhood. A lot of people said it was their first time setting foot on the campus. Founders Day has now been opened up to the public as well. It is all part of a continued change in philosophy to be more inclusive—of parents, of the community, and of new ideas.

During the 1960s and '70s enrollment dipped to around only 200 students as white flight occurred and low-income white families fled the downtown area and the newly integrated school. The demographics of the school changed along with the city.

Now, the school is overwhelmingly African American at 81 percent, with a smattering of whites and Hispanics, and has slightly more girls than boys with their largest enrollment in 2006, 720 students, since 1964. Tuition, which now comes to $37,000 per student, is still almost entirely paid for by the endowment, the rest through private donations.

The endowment was so large that for well over a hundred years the school didn't need to aggressively reach out to alumni or the corporate world for assistance. But as the buildings aged, repairs and renovations became necessary, the cost aggravated by inflation and growth. A grant for the new roof on Founder's Hall was the school's first attempt at obtaining funding from an outside foundation.

Thomas Baggio, who is director of development, which means chief fundraiser, came back to help his old home build a solid base of donors. It's only fitting that as Girard's vision has finally started to evolve, just a little, away from its founder's will, a new generation sees to the upkeep and makes plans for the future.

Plans are in the works to follow up with past and future graduates and track the alumni. No records are kept on alumni that shows who moved up to middle-class status or beyond, who successfully married and had children, or who went back to change anything about the dynamics of the neighborhood they came from.

There's no way of knowing if Girard's presence has affected the juvenile crime rate, if students are trying to improve themselves with an eye toward being admitted to Girard, if any of the alumni come back to where they began and attempt to rehabilitate their old block or start a new business. Even a school that began in 1848 has to continue to evolve, grow and stretch—just like the students—in order to continue being successful.

Besides the new roof, there is a new elementary school and dorms, built by the same company in 2001, that blend in nicely with the old buildings while offering modern conveniences like central air conditioning and keeping out the squirrels.

Mr. Lavell and Mr. Davis, the two RAs, found that out the next morning. Mr. Davis came downstairs in Merchant Hall to find his charges running toward him as a pack, all jammed together. Every man for himself.

He braced himself for whatever menace was after them, and as the boys passed him he saw the culprit. A small squirrel.

Squirrels come in the large front doors, particularly the middle school boys' dorms, Merchant and Mariner Halls, and have gotten a little wise to the tricks to get them out. Although, a squirrel did find its way into a snack machine and needed an assist after a large nosh.

As the boys streamed past the old couches that line the walls and into Mr. Lavell's office and huddled, Mr. Lavell took charge and grabbed a trash can and lid. He was going to wrangle the squirrel and show the boys a thing or two about taking charge and being empowered. Mr. Davis stood by, watching with amusement.

Mr. Lavell cornered the squirrel and was moving in with the lid to gently lead the small rodent into the large trash can and successfully carry it outside. A hero saving the day. As he moved in closer, the squirrel, sensing the flanking on both sides, leaped toward the wall, made a nice Cirque de Soleil-like bounce, ricocheted off of the other wall and leaped toward Mr. Lavell. Toward Mr. Lavell's head to be exact.

Suddenly, Mr. Lavell was running down the hall, the trash can abandoned, the boys and Mr. Davis cracking up. Eventually, the squirrel saw itself out.

They're still chuckling about it at breakfast. Mr. Lavell retelling the story with just the right amount of derring-do before breaking into laughter. It's a nice little anecdote about good intentions sometimes going awry and being able to laugh at yourself. It is yet another necessary skill to accomplish change, and in evidence at each of the homes.

However, unlike other REFs, the students at Girard are selected from narrower margins. Students must show they can maintain a 2.0 average while at the school, have no discernible learning disabilities that would require special accommodations, and a certain modicum of behavior or they will be asked to leave, and every year some are sent home, although efforts are made to help a child stay on track. Any child at Girard must also have a desire to be there. Unlike most other homes, no child can be placed there. Tamara Hoch, director of admissions, does her best to weed out the children who are just trying to please their parents. That has kept their attrition rate relatively low at 11 to 13 percent.

The grading scale is typical of affluent suburbs with an A scoring from 93 to 100, a B at 85 to 92, a C at 77 to 84. Below that at Girard doesn't really matter. Most of these kids are in the A to B range.

Across the campus from the upper school buildings, separated by short distances, is the elementary school, offices, and dorms. Elizabeth Becker is in her second year as the principal of the elementary school. She grew up in Philadelphia and went to nearby Chestnut Hill College but was unaware as a kid that Girard even existed. Hershey School was the place her mother used to threaten to send her brother. It's not all that unusual for exasperated parents to mistakenly portray whatever REF is nearby as the bogeyman. Unfortunately, though, it only adds to the misconceptions that the children aren't well-cared for or treated with kindness, respect, and love.

Miss Becker's original career plan was to stay at Girard for just a year and then head to the suburbs where there was real money to be made. She started as a math teacher, and then ten years later became a temporary principal till they could find someone else. Becker turned out to be the right fit.

We head to the cafeteria for lunch with the second and third graders, passing a small troop of first graders along the way. One of them excitedly calls out to Miss Becker about the much-anticipated birth of baby chicks. The little people don't know it, but there's no place for most of the chicks to go to once they're hatched. Avian flu has made it impossible to just give them away. It makes the adults give a small grimace every time one of the children delights in the approaching arrivals. Things look grim for the chickens. Fortunately, there are guinea pigs and their unexpected offspring and baby fish which will be around for a lot longer.

On the menu in the cafeteria is chicken fingers and Jell-O. The room is crowded with children busy getting their trays, chatting, catching up on the day. Miss Becker and I sit at a crowded round table with the kids. I pose a question to the small boy on the left, "Do you like being here?"

"I hate it here," he said, his voice full of passion. "I said I wanted to come here because my mother wants me to get a good education." Almost as quickly, his face relaxes and he changes the subject. "My uncle said he's going to make me a basketball star. I have a tall cousin." He's talking faster and faster telling me about cousins and buddies in his nearby neighborhood and his mom. He is weaving around himself the network of people that make up his life.

"He's going to be fine," says Miss Becker, leaning in to say it quietly. "He's still adjusting to being here, but he's got a lot of loving support behind him."

On the other side of Miss Becker is a little girl and I pose the same question.

"I won't be here next year," she says with a little bit of emphasis and relief. "My mom said so."

Miss Becker tenses a little, and waits till the child has gone to take her tray back. "That isn't true," she says. "Her mother isn't telling her the truth and has told her that to make life easier for herself this summer."

The boy and girl are both showing strong signs of being homesick but from two different angles. Contrasting examples of good and bad parenting. The young boy will go on to adjust to Girard, while dreaming of playing basketball and figuring out some other talents as he learns to build trusting and healthy relationships with all of the adults in his life.

The girl is going to have a hard moment come August when she is driven back through the gates at Girard and realizes what the truth has been all along. It will make not only the teachers' and RAs' job harder but every other adult she interacts with because the thought will be there. Do they have their own agenda? Can I trust?

That can make it hard to ask for help, to allow in new ideas, and to stretch out into unknown and different territory.

Miss Becker stands up and lets the children know they have only a few minutes left to eat and then it will be time to take up their trays and head back to class. An older girl, a third grader with blonde pigtails, ignores the warning and flits off to chat first with one friend then another, leaving most of her lunch untouched. Time passes and all of the trays are taken back, including hers. At the last moment she returns and notices the empty spot.

"Where's my tray?" she asks.

"It's been returned. It's time to go," says Miss Becker, firmly but with no judgment attached. This is just a consequence, not a comment on character.

The child hesitates only a moment before giving a small shrug. "Okay," she says and heads off with the other children.

No whining about fairness, no pleading about hunger, not even a good grimace. In the burbs where I come from and at every theme park I've ever visited, there is a lot of daily pleading, moment to moment pleading, about a lot of different boundaries. Chores, showing up on time, doing homework, watching less TV, going to bed on time, brushing all the teeth—not just the ones in front. There's an endless list. Mash that together with a tired parent who's distracted by bills or a bad cholesterol count but wants their child to have more than they did. Whew. It can get tough to separate out what's best for the child and just do it. That's one of the clear advantages Girard has going for it. There's forethought put into every action with the intention of teaching each child that not only is the sky the limit but to reach higher with the expectation of responsibility, independence, and success. Not just success.

It's a lot more empowering and stops the futile behavior of judging ourselves based on what someone else, an outside source, thinks because we think we're dependent on them in order to achieve a goal. There's a small group of us in our forties and fifties trying very diligently to unlearn that life lesson right now and at times it has seemed like a scary proposition.

Trust yourself, and trust yourself so much you know how to ask for help.

In the afternoon Mrs. Bowman's third graders head to the music room with their clear, electric green recorders to learn the song, "Merrily We Roll Along." There are playful foot stomps at every stop in the song before moving ahead.

"If you drop your recorder, that's a grade," says Dmytro Terleckyj, their music teacher. He's talking about the behavior grade. His tone is stern, but kind, and there's a definite expectation of following instructions. Slowly the tune plays out in recognizable fashion.

Up next, it's the first graders' turn. The small girls are in plaid smocks with white peter pan collars and burgundy knee socks. The boys are in grey slacks, white golf shirts, burgundy sweaters, and black shoes. They sit, very attentive, as their music teacher, Paul Eaton, quizzes them about what note they've just heard. Every time they get the note right he rewards them by playing a drum solo.

"Free dance!" he yells, and the children pop up, dancing feverishly, until he suddenly stops drumming, their signal to sit back down, grins everywhere. He plays another note and hands shoot up, hoping for another solo.

Over in the high school building, Rick Leek, a fifty-year-old history teacher, heavy set with a bushy grey moustache, is leading a group of twelve junior girls through the Kennedy era. The girls are attentive, sitting forward in their chairs, watching him as he strides back and forth across the worn wood floor in front of them, speaking in a heavy Philly accent, stopping occasionally behind a lectern.

He is shooting questions at them and they are all eagerly raising their hands, wanting to be chosen. Facts are backed up by stories, and dates easily roll out as he jokes easily with the kids. It's his daily stage, open mic several periods a day.

The classroom is old school with a chalk board surrounded by an impressive wooden frame, wide planked floors, and built-in glass-fronted bookcases. It all has a certain grace that age and push pin holes don't take away. There are photos of different places around the world ringing the front of the room, topped off with a signed photo of a bespectacled Bill Cosby, a fellow native of Philadelphia, at the end.

The hallways outside the room with its tall door, topped by a transom and brass handle, are wide with high ceilings dotted with insulated panels and old smoke alarms. Downstairs, yellow lockers line the opposite wall with flags of different countries hanging above the radiators. The school colors spread out in a diamond pattern across the floor.

It is appropriate in a building that reflects the past settling in with the present that there are banners all the way down the middle school hall, full of names of the past. Class of 1995 leads it off with their hand-prints and names. So much potential has moved through here.

Up one floor on the high school corridor there are cases along several walls that hold a vast array of stuffed birds and animals of every size from a mouse to a crocodile and includes a giant lobster, a blacktail jackrabbit, a domestic cat, and a lot of muskrats. Three cases are devoted to birds with over a hundred small songbirds and a large King Bird of Paradise, its feathers splayed. No one can remember if the objects were donated or a long-forgotten homework assignment for an entire grade. John Romano, the biology teacher, likes to use the cases when he's teaching about evolution. The middle schoolers think it's the cool kind of creepy.

Dr. Jeffrey Brown, the middle school principal, is giving a quick tour of the entire building. He has been at Girard for thirteen years and before that spent seventeen years at a private correctional school for boys who had committed serious crimes, including rape or robbery. Girard's long hours don't bother him. He has a unique perspective.

"Our biggest problems here are chewing gum and the kids not having their shirts tucked in their pants," he said. The lapel on his jacket

A classroom at Girard.

is lined with small pins including a "Bon Jour" pin left over from a Founders Day celebration. His office is littered with knickknacks: small statues, a beautiful but battered brass menorah, globes, flags, and the expected small bust of Girard, his later years. There is even a little glass cube of soldiers in dressage.

Over in Miss Gaillard's eighth-grade Spanish class a group of boys are playing Loteria, Spanish bingo, using corn kernels to fill in the spaces on the cards. They're learning common phrases. Learning a foreign language, French or Spanish, is a requirement, as set down by Girard's will. Girard was a native of France and came to Philadelphia by way of New Orleans.

Young men, in what many think of as a "difficult age" are quietly placing corn kernels on a sheet, hushing each other, keeping each other in line. There is a mutual balance of respect at the school that starts from the top down. The teachers, the RAs, the administrators don't ask anything of the kids that they don't expect from themselves. And the expectations are high.

Surprisingly, the stress levels are low. It's assumed that things will work out okay. Granted, the children who attend Girard start out with less baggage than most of the kids at a place like the Virginia Home. There are no social services kids here, for example, and therefore no one who has been through several foster homes first. And, with a higher academic standard there is none of the painful angst that can come from trying to teach a child with learning disabilities, or helping the child who is intelligent but not getting things as easily as everyone else build self-esteem.

≈≈

I know about that pain. I've lived it as a parent. Everyone who has ever met Louie has commented on how charming and intelligent he is. It was fun when he was ten to watch grown men claim they knew something about a basketball or football team and listen as Louie asked them a barrage of questions about particular players or strategies or statistics. His mental encyclopedia of knowledge was impressive from the start, and the listener's eyes would widen as they realized they'd been called out. But learning in general was more difficult for him because of his ADD, dyslexia, and dysgraphia.

School and Louie was an issue from the start, but the problem really grew beginning in the second grade. He had a wonderful teacher, Mrs. Kelly, who was patient and kind and took Louie in stride, but he wasn't happy.

Taking Louie in stride, at times, was saying a lot. To cover up the moments when he couldn't follow what everyone was doing, like reading in class, Louie made jokes and worked hard at getting the other kids to laugh—a typical method used by kids with learning disabilities of any kind. He spent a considerable hunk of second grade standing outside of the class, patiently waiting till he could go back inside.

"Don't worry about it, Louie," I said. "I spent my share of time sitting out in hallways. I was a big chatter and I turned out fine." I was attempting to cover a gaping wound with a band-aid.

And underneath it all, Louie was growing more and more unhappy. The differences between himself and all of his friends was becoming more apparent to him and he was making unfavorable comparisons but keeping it all to himself. However, pain has a way of leaking out the sides. Louie came home from school almost every day complaining about how much he hated it.

"I don't like it. I hate it there," he'd say, his face full of anguish.

"Why?"

"I don't know. I just don't."

It was all he ever said. There were little clues he dropped from time to time, like how much he was being berated by different teachers for inattention, some of them making it personal.

To keep a better eye on Louie and intervene as much as I could I volunteered to be a class mother every year he was in elementary school and went on as many field trips as possible. I knew getting to know me would make it harder for teachers or other parents to gossip about Louie and it was easier to step in and help Louie out without anyone noticing why I needed to.

"Quiet down now, time to get started. Everyone, turn toward your computer screen," said the librarian. We were in a small, narrow room off of the library that had computers along the entire wall and a few in the middle. Louie, now in second grade, sat at one across the room, facing the librarian. I was the volunteer mother for computer class.

I stood quietly behind him and pressed my hand down on his shoulder without looking directly at him. He stopped fidgeting and looked up at me. I nodded toward the screen and then the librarian.

He looked up at her as if he had just become aware of her.

"Click on the program we were using on Tuesday," she said, looking around the room. Louie moved his mouse and started working. I was the only one who was aware Louie wasn't always able to discern her voice from anyone else's.

"Thank you for volunteering," said the librarian, as the children got ready to leave. "It's such a big help," she said, smiling.

"Happy to do it," I said, waving to Louie as he filed out of the room.

Every time I ran into another mother, Pauline, who also had a son in the second grade, at the grocery store and heard what new horrible thing was being tried on her delightful son who also had learning disabilities I'd resolve all over again to never spill a word about Louie's inability to read, even to Louie, and I kept reading to him.

He let this new facet blend right into all of the rest of what defined us and I kept the truth about Louie to myself and said nothing. The outward appearance looked fine. But Louie was gradually forming a picture of himself as broken.

I wasn't looking for the little puzzle pieces, and that made it easier to ignore the picture they were forming. Watching him suffer, though, was too much. I had to do something.

I tried to solve it by restructuring Louie's school, or really, unstructuring it.

In my defense, I have wonderful memories of high school and thought they were so wonderful that of course everyone else, particularly a child of mine, would have a similar experience. And, I further reasoned (and reasoning is usually what got me in trouble when it came to Louie), that even if his experience was not quite up to mine it would still be wonderful, mine having been so great.

I didn't consult anybody about my theories or conclusions because that would have required letting someone in on the big secret about Louie. He couldn't read. He was also having difficulty following directions, keeping anything he owned in some semblance of order, or paying attention, but I downplayed these signs as well. I was so afraid of what others might think or do that I didn't consider it would be possible to stay put in public school, work honestly with misguided people, and still come up with workable solutions.

Living in my own confusion, trying to do what was *best* for Louie, I took him out of public school, away from the potential labels and his unhappiness, and put him in the third grade at a local Montessori school. I thought that its open structure and move-at-your-own-pace attitude would suit Louie better. He'd feel more in control of his situation and grow happier. Imagine my surprise when the opposite happened.

In Louie's new world of people moving in different directions at will he was expected to keep order and progress on his own. His little cubby quickly became perpetually crammed with papers, and he was always behind on the little marks that said what was completed. He seemed blissfully unaware of both but kept a constant feeling of general anxiety.

The first year he attended the school, things were a little better, but not because of the school. A new student, Araceli Molina, a beautiful, brown-haired girl from Mexico City, was in the states for a year with her younger brother, Juan, while her mother, Silvia, studied and worked at Medical College of Virginia and their father, Juan Carlos, a family practitioner, looked for something to do.

Louie, at age nine, was immediately smitten by this tall reed of a girl with large brown eyes and followed her everywhere, doing all of the talking for both of them. He was so smitten he didn't notice she didn't speak English for months, which by that time she had learned enough of to start speaking up for herself. She had learned the language by listening to Louie.

I heard about it first from Louie's teacher, Jonathan, who was young and idealistic and adored by the kids. Before that job he worked in South America doing good deeds.

He pulled me aside with such a grin on his face to tell me about how the two stuck together, Louie always carefully making sure Araceli was taken care of. Sounded good, looked good at first, but Louie was aping my mistakes, doing everything for someone else like I did for him, rather than watch them struggle and possibly feel bad about themselves. Fortunately, Araceli was low maintenance, which meant she was her own person and didn't need propping up, and when she could say stop, she did. Louie by then was enchanted and was happy to let go of some of the reins.

Louie finally told me about Araceli one night and I held my breath, listening to my only child grow up and pull away just a little. I knew there were still years to go, but I could feel the first steps away from me.

"I knew I like, liked her from the first time I saw her because she made me feel sweaty and dizzy," he said. Pretty accurate description of how someone can make you feel, I thought.

My first good look at the two of them together was at an Earth Day celebration, which if you know anything about Montessori, is a big deal. There was food and exhibits and a small band playing as the all-day celebration moved along.

In the midst of it, Louie asked Araceli to dance, giving me a glimpse of the Louie from before school ever entered the picture.

"Want to dance?" he said, offering his hand. She gave the smallest hint of a smile, looking at him through her long, dark eyelashes and put her hand in his. They slowly glided around the room without effort or pretense. Louie was going on ahead of me again, showing me the path, lighting it up for me.

Neither one of them was embarrassed to be dancing in front of their classmates, even though they were the only ones dancing. When the music was over, they moved on to another activity. It was all so simple.

The last night Araceli was in this country we all had dinner together, the Molina-Cruzes and the Carrs at Araceli's rented townhouse in a development surrounded by strip malls and the parking lot of a YMCA. We ate what Louie called Mexican pizzas at the blue card table and chairs they were leaving behind for me to take home. After dinner, we played our usual raucous game of Uno. Five-year-old Juan kept all of his cards on the table, face up, and still beat us, as usual.

It came time to leave and the two of them could barely look at each other. They mumbled goodbye as Louie and I walked toward my old white Chevy. Araceli and her mother stood in the doorway waving goodbye.

At the car Louie turned and before their door shut and the moment was lost, he ran back to Araceli and kissed her on the cheek, not waiting for a response. He moved quickly to the car, taking long strides, pulled open the stubborn, heavy door and slid inside.

We left Montessori behind and Louie went back to public school. He was now in the fifth grade, and struggling. I read to him, discussed history and science with him, helped him with elaborate projects and cajoled him through the grade, but the misery was settling in deeper.

The next year was spent in public middle school and was more of the same marked by more days when Louie came home miserable than not. Teachers were occasionally making comments on his report cards about his goofing around in class, speaking out, and trying to get the other kids to laugh, but that was it. We were all in on the great illusion together.

Nothing got better. Louie spent most of the year begging me to find another school for him to try someplace else. He liked most of his teachers, got along well with enough of the kids, and hated going to school every single day. Everything felt like an enormous effort.

But I had made Louie a promise when he was born to always look after him, and I was going to keep trying to get it right. I filled out an application for the local private Episcopal boys' school, St. Christopher's, and turned to the old family ties to get numerous prominent names to put in a good word for Louie. It was all going great, until I had to take Louie in for testing.

It was a two-day affair with a little bit of everything. Vocabulary, math, and writing skills. Louie went down in flames.

"Look at his essay," said the woman in charge of testing. She was speaking in a very gentle tone. "One paragraph doesn't follow the other and he didn't really answer the question. None of it really makes sense. By his grade, we expect a more cohesive essay."

I sat there nodding my head, trying to think of some way to spin this so that Louie could still be admitted, saved, but there was nothing to be said.

"It would be unfair to your son to place him here," she said. "We move at a very fast pace and he would fall behind. He'd be miserable."

'But, but …' I was thinking, but I already knew she was right. I took the papers and drove home slowly, trying to figure out how I was going to tell Louie.

He was watching television in the family room.

"Okay," trying to sound light and breezy as I sat down on the couch. "It doesn't look like St. Christopher's is going to work out, but there are a couple of other places we can try."

"Why?"

"Why what?"

"Why can't I go there?" Louie wasn't going to let me glide over this one.

"Well, the testing didn't have the results they hoped for, but you were tired and rushed. There are other schools," I added quickly, trying to move the topics along. Louie wasn't having any of it.

"They didn't want me?" his voice was rising in anger and hurt. "What, did I fail?"

"No," I said, lying to both of us, "but they have a list of criteria and they felt their school wasn't the right place for you. There are other schools we can apply to." I was determined not to use the word, fail, and was in full-blown denial. Somehow, I reasoned, if I don't admit it Louie can't sink his teeth into it either. But all I was doing was leaving him to reason his way to a feeling of failure and being completely alone. I obviously wasn't going to talk about it, so he wasn't going to get the chance to either.

All those labels I was trying to avoid, and I couldn't see Louie was coming up with even darker ones to apply to himself.

We applied to another private school.

Louie had to take a long standardized test and did reasonably well on it, which he could do—depending on the test and how he felt that day. Fortunately, we had hit on a good day. His elementary school grades looked fine—because I was reading to him and talking with him so much—and Montessori didn't really give grades, so we looked at least acceptable on that score. He had to do some testing with an educational consultant who pointed out he couldn't comprehend much of what he read, but I spun that into just a little glitch that I was sure could be improved upon in such a wonderful, shiny school with so many resources and those small classes.

We got in. I was so relieved, I would have grabbed at anything just to avoid telling Louie anyone else had stamped a 'no' on his forehead.

Louie joined the middle school basketball team and did his best to settle in to a routine. It was the worst experiment yet.

While Louie's ability to read did improve markedly, his ability to comprehend what he was reading didn't. So he could imitate the skill, but not get much out of it. We all applauded at the number of books he read and breathed a sigh of relief anyway. Back to hugging the illusion.

The smaller classes helped and the teaching method of lectures rather than reading hid the problem more effectively, but Louie couldn't pay attention or keep a complex order in his mind so there were holes, big ones. The second year he was there the math teacher despised Louie and let him know it, a lot. He couldn't get the steps in a problem straight and even though four out of five steps were correct, a lot of questions on the tests were marked completely wrong and he was failing the class. By now, Louie had grown a certain stubborn thick skin to the personal taunts from adults about his inattentiveness and he'd shut them out. He shut her out. He didn't turn in homework, made jokes to his friends when her back was turned and turned a bored face to her when she was looking straight at him. He was furious inside with no one to tell it to, and she fed the anger by telling him he was a problem, the class would be better off if he weren't in it. Not his behavior, *him.*

She tried to retaliate against his behavior in small, mean ways. Louie came back to school after being sick for days and she said he had sixty math problems to do in one night or he'd get a zero. I helped him finish them and spoke to the principal of the middle school. This battle was getting out of hand.

"I spoke to the teacher," said the principal, as we stood outside in the parking lot. "And I don't believe Louie. If I have to take a side, I always take the teacher's," he said. Louie was standing next to me, listening intently. "Louie's the problem here, not the teacher."

"So you're telling me that no child should ever expect you to stick up for them, and all a teacher has to do is tell you what you want to hear and you'll go for it."

"That's right," he said, firmly nodding his head, his lips pulled into a thin line. "My job is to represent the teachers."

The math teacher walked by, on her way to her car. He waved hello to her. "Would you like her to join us?" he asked.

"What would be the point of that?" I retorted.

Later, I wrote a letter to the school saying I didn't want Louie even in her classroom anymore, to please let him finish his work elsewhere, but they refused. I couldn't have a say in it. He had to endure her behavior and the blind eye of the school to the end of the year.

"You don't have to like this woman, Louie," I told him, "but unfortunately, you're going to have to be the adult in this case and quietly get through this. Whatever the grade is, we're letting it go. No worries. I'm sorry."

Louie headed back to public school for yet another try, and still without the necessary testing.

I had had my reasons, however misguided, for keeping the truth from everyone, including Louie. In the beginning when Louie was in kinder-garden, the principal was placing LD kids with mentally retarded kids because he saw no difference in *how* someone learns with *how much* someone can learn. But I carried it too far, until the ninth grade at Godwin High School and the kindly Mr. Ribble, when Louie stopped let-ting me help him. It's a testimony of how much he was trying to take care of my feelings that he let it go that far. Not a nice thing to have to admit.

After a short honeymoon period Louie caught on to how others, including a few teachers, saw people with permanent learning disabili-ties and his anger deepened. I didn't handle it well, despite my best efforts. I careened between too much help and hands off, never finding a sure footing. Sometimes, I wondered if this was where we started to slide and I just didn't really see it. If this was where our wall between the world of the suburbs and the homes became thin.

⨃⨃⨃

Sitting in the classrooms at Girard, watching these children, though, there was an absence of struggle.

The bingo game in Miss Gaillard's eighth grade Spanish class con-tinued with the kids trying to make different patterns of Xs or hori-zontal or vertical lines to get the chance to yell "Bingo" before the game moved on.

One young man, though, was quietly eating the raw, hard kernels as he watched everyone else play the game and call out.

Suddenly, Miss Gaillard noticed his page was blank and the kernels were nowhere to be seen. "Where is your corn?" she asked, incredulous.

"I ate them," he said, matter-of-factly.

"Why?" she said, wide-eyed. "How?"

He picked up another kernel, one of the last and was about to show her, at least the how. He was doing this without any snarky resentment or sass. He was apparently just bored and hungry.

"No, no," she said, hurriedly, stopping him in mid-swallow. "Okay, everybody, let's just gather up the corn and put it away before any more of it disappears."

The student stayed after to discuss the consequences of not participating and eating part of the game.

I looked back as I got ready to head to another classroom and saw Miss Gaillard speaking quietly to the student who was shrugging his shoulders. What was interesting to note, what I realized was different from a lot of other adult to child discussions I've witnessed, was the lack of shame or guilt.

It wasn't personal.

Everyone started from the premise that there were certain standards, which was basic no matter what school or home you're standing in, and that every child here can accomplish whatever task is asked of them. It inspires respect and a calm.

That's what had tripped me up in my own parenting. I was attached to the outcome not sure of what that might be, and it was obvious in my questions, pleading, doubts. It didn't help that both Louie and I were part of a long line of over-achievers and without knowing it I had interpreted perfection over excellence as a standard. Achievement as a mark of worth.

A small truth I have kept inside, trying to push it away.

Walking around Girard I had been reviewing every parenting decision I ever made, every moment with my son, and wondering what I could have done differently. My son's anger has only grown since his grandfather's death, and I have wondered how I can make up for the past, even though I know there are a thousand good memories and there's nothing more I could have done. Every moment of Louie's life I was doing the absolute best I could.

And, now it seemed as if I have failed. I wasn't strong enough or detached enough or sure enough. There are a lot of enoughs. And with every one I know immediately that they aren't true, but standing here looking at these children who are thriving, absent of angst, much less anger, I wonder again. The pain is so real I feel like it is visible to everyone who looks at me, but maybe not.

I meet another RA, Terry Powell, tall and lean with long braids pulled back in a loose ponytail. She is in her late twenties and possesses a calm and assurance that is infectious. She is in her fifth year at the school, and I ask her how long she expects to work there. She answers with a story, about how long she resisted being right there. Resisted working with the girls, the wall of sound, and was burning out. How much she missed being like other twenty-somethings who could leave work and just hang out at a restaurant with their friends or head off to a movie on a whim.

"What changed?"

"I stopped wishing I was someplace else," she said, giving me the same even smile. "I decided to be happy." Happy by choice with what is, rather than some dream that just isn't. Not happy because the circumstances accidentally happened to fall into place. Miss Powell wasn't giving up on a dream; she was starting to see the value in what she already had.

It is as if something had started to dislodge from within. Maybe it was possible for me to see and celebrate who Louie is, who I am, and let go of an illusion. Free myself from the fear of something I couldn't quite name, though still the larger force in my life.

Walking through the campus that night I passed through a crowd of seniors jostling each other, trading jokes, and whispering back and forth.

The sun is just about to set and everything is in shadow against the very white blossoms of the trees. The students move around me easily and keep talking as if I'm not there. It feels like a compliment, like I've been accepted as at least harmless, and they continue on in the language they reserve for each other. A language all teenagers have that they generally hide from adults.

Founders Hall is still imposing in the darkness, with its wide, white

Students relaxing on the grounds.

stone steps still visible as I pass by. A lot of the buildings on campus are historical landmarks of the kind that make a statement.

A recent movie about Annapolis was filmed here, the large columns and green walkways easily passing for the Naval Academy grounds. The school earned a nice fee filling in for the academy and in every preview as the camera pans back the chapel's roof is neatly displayed before the scene switches to actors in uniforms standing on the steps of Founders Hall, the original school building.

The structure of Founders Hall is lovingly detailed in directions left by Girard including "it shall be fire proof inside and outside. The floors and the roof to be made of solid materials, on arches turned on proper centres [*sic*], so that no wood may be used, except for doors, windows and shutters." It was the second most expensive building in the country by the time it was finished.

The same architect who designed the Capitol dome designed

Founders Hall with those wide stone steps leading up to a very tall green door that opens with a shove from a shoulder onto a marble foyer.

Imagine all of the little hard-sole shoes clacking across the floor the past one hundred fifty years, echoing off of the two sweeping staircases on either side.

Each of the two former classrooms in the building are large with tall windows and hand-blown glass. The building is no longer used for classes but hosts the occasional reception. Weddings, or any other religious rites, are not permitted at Girard, in keeping with the will. Girard, who was Catholic and against organized religion, forbade not only any proselytizing of any kind, but also any religious figure from setting foot on the grounds. Thomas Baggio, director of development, is an alumnus of Girard, class of '59. He remembers what it was like when Girard played nearby Catholic schools. "The priest always had to sit on the wall," he said, laughing. "Their feet couldn't touch the ground." Lately, the rule has been relaxed to at least let priests or ministers on the grounds, but a recent speaker, who also happened to be a minister, was told beforehand that if any part of his speech sounded suspiciously like doctrine, his speech would be cut short.

In 2005, the school won a $544,554 grant from the Save America's Treasures Foundation and every cent went toward replacing the aging marble roof on Founders Hall with a new state-of-the-art roof that would be in keeping with the historic style while providing protection of all of the artifacts the building now contains. Other buildings are in need of similar expensive repairs.

There is a sense of permanence to all of the buildings that gives the grounds a calming effect. It doesn't hurt that the dogwoods are all in bloom and dot the campus everywhere standing beside old oak and maple trees with full, green branches.

The chapel is equally impressive with a tall, vaulted ceiling and housing a 7,000 pipe organ, the third largest in Philadelphia, a city known for its impressive churches. A new sound system has been added as a gift from the class of '53 along with a CD that plays the alma mater and chimes.

The original design for the chapel was even grander, but the Depression began and plans were scaled back. The money and marble that was left over was enough to build the library in 1935, the last building to be erected before the current campus-wide renovations. Everything in the library is still the original material, except the computers, tables, and books. Elaborate ceiling lamps hang down; some have lost their original covers and have been replaced with newer versions that look like cake toppers. Heavy fans dot the area fighting the humidity. None of the older buildings have been retrofitted with air conditioning.

"The huge dream now," said Frances Smith, head of the board of education, "is to have a new middle school building because we are cramped. The whole west wing of the Old Junior School that's being gutted, and the east side is being renovated; beautiful large rooms that could be renovated to classrooms."

The night is winding down. The girls, who are under Miss Mudry, are starting to get off of the Internet, wandering back toward their rooms.

The twins, Champagne and Charmaine, two outgoing brown-skinned girls with shapely curves whose moods are always ready to turn back to sunny, are discussing careers.

"I'd like to be a model, a singer, an actress, or a lawyer," says Champagne, the twin without braces. "What kind of lawyer makes the most money?" she asks, with a serious, determined tone.

The question is evidence of the power of an outline used by Marge Holmes, the middle school residential dean, to give kids more clarity about what it will take to reach their destinations in life.

Marge is a no-nonsense administrator who handles all of the behavioral problems that can pop up with boys and girls in the throes of puberty. The sagging couch outside of her office is almost always filled with a few bodies that need to chat about the "whys." Why they weren't where they were supposed to be? Why they were bothering someone else? Why they didn't get their chores done, again? There are a lot of whys in middle school.

The survey Marge uses as a tool to bring some reality into a life plan while goals are still so malleable asks children to start from the big picture. What do you want your life to look like? For kids, it's all about the household bling. Nice house, decent car, plenty of the latest gadgets in both.

"Okay," Marge says, in a strong Philly accent, to each student, who happily tells her what they expect out of life. "Let's add up what that's gonna cost."

Marge already knows she's got them as she adds up the thousands of dollars it will take to acquire and maintain the lifestyle they envision. Taxes are taken into account, along with a variety of necessary insurances. The number quickly grows till it hits well over a hundred grand. There are "oooohs" and "aaaahs" as the amount hits an area that is too large to comprehend in anything but the lifestyle.

The next step is to look at what professions can accommodate the income, which is where a lot of the girls in seventh grade spotted "lawyer." But it doesn't end there.

Now, Marge can point out what kind of commitment it will take in the present moment to eventually be able to be a lawyer or a doctor. She has done a neat little exercise with delayed gratification that is on the child's level. It's no longer about pleasing a parent or a teacher (the more short-term oriented approach), but about being able to acquire a life the students truly want. And, there's not only a path, there are people, guides, to help along the way.

Marge is in the process of hiring new RAs, which gives her the opportunity to ruminate about how far the program has come at Girard and what makes a good RA in the first place.

"We don't hire 'em," she says, "we create 'em. I want RAs who will give me 85 percent of their skills and talent." She is explaining the process that goes on to clarify for applicants how challenging this profession can be for anyone and how necessary it is to be realistic. In other words, a lot of jobs may only require half of your talents at any given moment with time for coffee or email or watering your potted plant. This one won't.

The impact of job performance on the children explains why Marge took it upon herself to redefine the job of residential advisor that used to be titled house parent—a title still standard in a lot of other homes.

"House parents in the dictionary of professional roles is much less defined. Now residential faculty; then you could change the competency. Then you could change the expectations," she said.

"I made it my mission that the field was going to be professionalized. I didn't understand why we couldn't have the same things as St. Andrew's," an elite boarding school. "The whole thing came to be about what it *could* be."

Since the changes in policy and pay raises that came along with it, Marge has been able to attract more college graduates to the openings. It's part of why she was named Administrator of the Year in 2005 by Coalition for Residential Education or CORE, the national umbrella organization in DC for residential education facilities.

One last story about *the wall of sound*. The girls, along with their RAs, Miss Robinson and Miss Powell, set out for roller skating in nearby Camden, New Jersey. A bus and driver were rented and off we went, a packed bus of middle school girls.

Inside, the rink was loud, so loud that it was hard to pick out words in the music. The girls quickly rented skates and set out around the wooden floor while the adults took up residence in a booth, watching them go around and around.

I took breaks from time to time to check on Louie, who wasn't answering, despite a new system of arranging a specific time. I had to let it go and rejoin the girls inside.

They were all busy having a good time, living in just that moment. Ashley, who was always as neat as a pin and smiling, skated all night long. Chantel struggled mightily to go all the way around the rink, but kept going anyway, only occasionally getting stuck in the middle. Lonaya, from northeast Philadelphia, who had the beautiful, long, braided hair extensions that were very popular in Philly then, skated easily in long fluid motions that seemed to be an extension of her spirit. Tyler, the artist from Upper Darby, who was small and wore glasses, looked like she wasn't having a good time. But as usual, if someone looked closer they would have found out that she was. And then, there was Nygeema, from Camden, who was the most powerful skater of the bunch, her broad shoulders squared as she moved easily and quickly around the rink, easily lapping the other girls.

They were a group of girls just like any other who took time out for pizza, day-glo light sticks and dancing under a light like they were on stage and in a girl group. For a moment, there were no worries. When it was finally time to get back on the bus and head back to Girard and home, tired, sweaty bodies piled on, giggling and whispering. The noise level ebbed and flowed like a tide, continuing as we pulled out of the parking lot and rode along dark streets. Occasionally, Miss Robinson or Miss Powell admonished them to quiet down.

Suddenly, the bus driver, a young man, stopped the bus and turned on the lights, announcing, "Quiet! Quiet! I will not move this bus until everyone is silent!"

Small titters of laughter floated up to the front as Miss Robinson rolled her eyes and Miss Powell rested her forehead on her hands, waiting for the driver to come to an understanding that is written in stone. Middle school girls aren't all that good at total silence late at night after a fun escape of roller skating, dancing, and pizza. Not going to happen. Minutes ticked by and there still wasn't the required absolute silence.

The bus driver, without acknowledging the truth behind the adage, *pick your battles*, quietly turned the interior lights off and got the bus under way. The *wall of sound* had worn him down.

I had spent those moments doing my best not to smile. It was a good reminder of what any kind of parenting can be at any given time. Most of us want to be great parents, and sometimes we are riding the wave easily, knowing just what to say and when to say it. And, at other times, we're crashing and getting everything wrong. Somehow, we get another chance and learn a little about humility as we turn the lights off and get back under way.

~~∽⌒∽~~

Before I left the campus to drive home along the east coast at night when the highway is clear, I called Louie to see how he was doing. He answered right away and said, "I'll see you when you get home," in a *pleasant* voice. "Love you." Sometimes, you ride the wave. "Love you, too," I said, and hung up before I could add any questions.

There was an interlude of peace after the visit to Girard during which I began to tell myself we were starting to take the curve, and everything will be all right. Illusion was still my stock in trade, but it didn't last. Not too many weeks after I got home, things changed and tested us again, as if all of those years of waiting in my parents' home had to be peeled away quickly.

However, just this once, a little grace, a little forgiveness found us.

Forgiveness is a very strange beast. We work at handing it out because we're told to; it'll make us better people. We do it reluctantly, dragging ourselves through the months or years it can take to feel the first slight tug of letting go. We do it slowly because the bursts of anger toward the one who did us wrong feels so good. For just that moment we feel powerful and in control, when maybe most of the time we don't.

For so long, I had carried around an anger toward my ex-husband, my only child's father, like a prized possession. Taking it out and polishing it to a shiny glow just often enough to keep the anger at a slow burn. I felt justified because of the constant chaos brought on by his sudden departure. Then, there were the repeated arguments over child support, and yet one more trip to court. Bailiffs greeted me by name while I waited for yet another court appearance, sitting on the yellow pine benches outside the courtroom doors. They knew I was a writer, had taken up running, asked me how my parents were doing. I saw them that often.

"I have a right to be angry," I said.

But here's the catch. Holding on to the anger and the hurt had left me frozen in that spot, forever circling. It was anger as a thin veneer over a deeply buried fear. A fear that I couldn't take care of myself or my son. That I lacked an essential gene that told everyone else how to get the right job, figure out a budget, find a good mate.

But focusing on the hurt was so much easier than facing any truths about myself. And besides, every time I took out the laundry list of things my ex-husband had done over the years, the look of astonishment across their faces encouraged me.

"That was awful. How did you stand it? Boy, you must be happier now."

I *was* happier in the day-to-day moments without someone yelling at me or criticizing. Sometimes I stood still just to listen to the silence, a smile building on my face.

But the doubts remained, and to cover it up I gained weight. A lot of weight. I topped out at close to 300 pounds before working hard to get all of it off through the old fashioned routine of diet and exercise.

I wrote about it all, exorcised the demons, trained to run a marathon, finished 23 miles of it, felt good and moved on.

Or so I hoped.

The traces of anger, the old feelings of somehow being wronged, lingered deep within. I had worked on the outside hoping the inside would take care of itself.

Louie was by then thirteen years old, with five years left to go till my ex and I could sever the ties more deeply and finally let go. It felt like a sharp stone in the pit of my belly. Half of the pain from anticipating what he would do next that I could add to the list. Half from wondering whether once the child support was gone, if would I be able to cope on my own (not necessarily cope financially but without the ties to an old bad habit).

Slowly I put back on some of the weight, congratulating myself that it was only half of what I had lost—a minor victory—being way too hard on myself that I couldn't keep up the same training schedule I had when I was training for a marathon. All or nothing—another excuse—and for awhile I chose to do nothing.

It took another year before I grew tired enough to want to change, and this time change everything.

A very wise minister, Rev. Thelma Smith from the Spiritual Mind Center, said: "Start from where you are. Say, 'I forgive the dumb bastard,' if that's where you are and let it go. Let that be enough for now if that's all you have." What she meant was, quit waiting for optimal conditions to even set out at all.

I must have said those five words hundreds of times a day, at first grimacing but eventually smiling at the words. Maybe that was progress. I said it as I started walking around my neighborhood, working up to a faster walk and then a little bit of running. But this time, there was a difference to all of it. It wasn't a test I was trying to pass to prove something to myself. It was okay if today I had to stop for a moment or took a shorter route. It was okay if today I said the words through clenched teeth. It was okay.

And then, in a moment, a phone call, we took that turn, and things changed again and I saw the blessing in it all. Louie called me on the phone from his father's, his voice catching, barely able to get out the words.

"Dad pleaded guilty to fraud today. He has to go to prison for over a year." Twenty-one months for something he did over five years ago. There had been no trial and he had kept it to himself till he knew all of the details.

And suddenly, the list vanished.

I know our son was bracing himself for whatever comeback I was going to say, but instead I surprised both of us.

"I'm proud of your dad," I said. "He's taking responsibility for what he did and handling it all the best he can." Imagine that.

We all mess up, I added, sometimes more spectacularly than others. It's how we handle the mess that shows our true character. Every ounce of worry left me in that moment and it felt like everything would be okay, for all three of us. None of it mattered anymore. We all got to be seen as human with our triumphs and our pitfalls.

I called his dad and we talked, a rare thing, and I told him I'd do my best to make sure Louie visited and wrote. He never once backed away from his responsibilities, even volunteering he'd make sure his part of the child support would be taken care of before he had to report.

It was only later that I realized something else. Being able to let go of the list—the past—made it possible for me to see the truth I had turned away from for so long. I was the one I needed to forgive all along. All of the guilt and wrong decisions, and standards of perfection. My ex was only my long-standing excuse.

There, at the end of the road of forgiveness, I didn't find the person who did me wrong, I found a reflection of myself, and in that moment I healed that part of me.

But, there are some things in this world that can't be controlled or cured, only recognized and dealt with, and Louie and I hadn't done that yet. Not with everything. I was still trying to put one foot in front of the other without allowing for the possibility that sometimes, crashing is a good thing. Eventually, this illusion, this last great illusion, would feel like it could crush both of us.

Chapter 3

The Calling

The story of Happy Hill Farm Academy, Granbury, Texas, founded in 1975 by Ed Shipman

My barn having burned to the ground, I can now see the moon.

Japanese Haiku

JASON'S STORY

*P*erspective is defined in the dictionary as the ability to perceive things from different sides and in their relative importance to the situation. It seems a lot of what people are arguing about when it comes to residential education facilities is a matter of their perspective.

Everyone wants every child to feel loved, nurtured, empowered, but what's the best way to get to that point, especially when the traditional familial bonds have been broken?

Perhaps, the best source to begin with when wondering about the viability of residential homes are those who have recently graduated from them. They have the advantage of living inside the different perspectives.

"Some of the homes we come from, that's the place you don't want to be. It's a blessing to come to a place like Happy Hill Farm Academy," said Jason Lamers, now thirty who graduated from Happy Hill in 1994 and has gone on to be a very enthusiastic public affairs officer for the mayor of the city of Forth Worth, not too far from the farm. "I'm so glad to work at a place like this and have some say on what goes on, and the mayor, Mike Moncries, is absolutely the greatest dude to work for that I've ever met. He's so real and that's what makes him so special," said Jason.

Joy and enthusiasm shape how Jason sees the world, whether he's talking about his wife of seven years, Kelli, or his young daughter, Chloe, who is two. It would be easy to assume that he must have started out that way, one of those lucky few who came to the planet seeing the bright side of everything. It would also make it easier to put him in a separate category from other alumni, make his perspective an exception.

But you'd be wrong. "Before I came to Happy Hill, I was a thug basically, running around on my skate board all day. I was a brat. I was twelve years old and I was heading down the wrong path and I just thought the world revolved around me," he said. A second chance came from his grandparents who drove past the farm occasionally and saw the place as a possible salvation for all four of their grandchildren. But that doesn't mean that the transition was a smooth one or that Jason didn't resist.

Shortly after he got to the farm, Jason ran away.

"I was asleep at a gas station and the police picked me up. Mr. Shipman picked me up from the police station." After a two-week time-out in his room during extracurricular activities where he had plenty of time to think about what he'd done, he decided to give just an inch and see where it'd take him.

It helped to change the perspective when he found out people were genuinely concerned about him. "Chuck Shipman talked to me. They were worried about me. I was surprised to find out that, now, I'm being held accountable and people are telling me they're worried about me.

"I was in a home where my mother was battling all kinds of addictions. She had me and my three other siblings and we were just running wild and my dad worked so much as a car salesman we rarely saw him except on Sundays," he said.

"My parents had me when they were twenty years old and didn't know what was going on, and my father put all of his time into getting food on the table.

"Happy Hill Farm was a life-changing experience. Ed Shipman is a God-send, it's amazing," he said. "He is an angel to all of us kids there. He totally saved my life. There's no way I'd be serving the mayor of the 18th largest city in America if it weren't for Ed Shipman and Happy Hill Farm."

There's a gap there, however, from where he started to who he is now. It took years, but finally in his junior year at the farm things started to click and he saw everything from a new place, creating a new perspective.

"I realized that these people knew what they were doing. All of these sporting events and extracurricular activities, I never would have been involved in any of them and maybe not even school. I began to see the long-term benefits of discipline, respecting your elders." All of this, he believes, prepared him for the pressures of the job he loves, making it easier for him to be grateful rather than lament.

And, as often happens, when one person's perspective changes, others follow. Jason's father used the opportunity having his children at Happy Hill gave him and went back to school to earn a degree and is now a teacher. Jason's sister who also graduated from the farm is now an art teacher. His other two siblings who left early and remained with their mother after his parents divorced are struggling. But Jason is there passing on what he learned from the farm, patiently letting them know there's another way to see things and it can change your life.

"I wrote Ed Shipman a thank you note after I graduated and it was kind of like *It's a Wonderful Life*, because think of how many lives were changed because there is an Ed Shipman.

"We can do anything we want to if we just have the faith," said Jason, "and I'm living proof that it can happen."

"Choose to be in close proximity to people who are empowering, who appeal to your sense of connection to intention, who see the greatness in you, who feel connected to God, who live a life that gives evidence that Spirit has found celebration through them."

Wayne Dyer, *The Power of Intention*

On a hill in north Texas sits the children's home, Happy Hill Farm Academy, nestled an hour and a half away from the big city of Dallas down a long straight highway dotted by newly built gas pipelines, scrub trees, churches, and new construction. Over a hundred children from kindergarten through the twelfth grade from all over Texas live at the farm with an average stay of two years. Visible from the road is a small village, still growing, and self-contained on 260 acres of a 500-acre plat. It's a small ranch by Texas standards. Homes of various sizes, along with a neat row of low one-story cottages, dot the slowly rising hill flanked in front and back by buildings necessary to keep a town going. To the left sits a small stocked lake and to the far

The entrance to Happy Hill Farm.

right the gym and agriculture buildings. All brought together by a man with a vision.

Ed Shipman, the founder of Happy Hill, will read this entire book and say God was the force behind everything that has happened. He will read this chapter and see reflected back all of his accomplishments and take credit for none of them. God will get all of the credit. If pressed, he will mention who God was working through to help carry out the mission: teachers, donors, different volunteers. He still won't include himself. God had the plan and Ed was his grateful servant. End of story.

Just reading that, it's possible to overlay all sorts of assumptions and suspicions. Bring in your own beliefs and decide ahead of time who Ed is and what he thinks of others, what categories he might place you in.

But, then, you'd miss the best part. Once you've met Ed, it doesn't take long before the first leaps of logic have failed, replaced quickly by another, which also falls by the wayside. If you stay around just long enough, everything will fall away until the only leap left is one of faith.

That's where this project started to take a turn that at first I wasn't willing to make and resisted, insisting this was supposed to be a story about others. An informational book—no memoir quality—stick to the facts.

But if I was going to keep any semblance of my good mother title, I was going to have to try to start listening and become part of the story. This is where the book started to morph into the answer to a prayer I said from the bottom of my soul, right after Dad died so unexpectedly. The signs were becoming harder to ignore.

"Dear God," I said, out loud like the beginning of a letter. I think it was because I was so unused to coming up with any original prayers. I was used to relying on something written by someone else a long time ago. "Please find a way to let me know I'm loved by You. Find a way to let me know so that I'll never doubt it again." I answered the prayer with a "thank you" and was tempted to add, "this is Martha."

I said the prayer before I knew what was about to happen with Louie, and set out on a journey. I didn't know how much I'd need it until the journey was almost over.

Ed was the second part of my answer. The first had been my willingness to even take on this project, and stick with it even when the question of how to get to the different locations or pay the bills while I did wasn't answered. I just kept going, relying on faith, which was a new muscle for me.

I didn't know that when I first met Ed I was about to get a better understanding that was going to allow me to finally get the next piece of the puzzle as to why these homes succeed, despite what the rest of us have seen as enormous obstacles. I had been steadily gaining pieces from each home, each teacher, and each child along the path.

What I saw when I first met Ed was a very determined, faith-based man who welcomed every positive idea, good or otherwise, that anyone had to offer. He'd lean in, cocking his head to one side, giving the impression he was really listening to each word, and wait till the person was finished before giving some sort of reply to let it be known that he got it. If the idea had merit it was put into motion right away.

And, whenever anyone tried to complain in Ed's presence, maybe they weren't even speaking directly to him, but tried to moan about their fate, Ed would physically turn away, and put up an arm, stretched out straight in front of him, as if he were willing even the energy of disappointment or *woe is me* to go away. It never took long for people stuck in blame or victimhood to go looking for a new audience.

It also never took very long for anyone who was willing to change to start to blossom. Fortunately, I was in that group, I just didn't realize how much, yet, and I was reluctant at first to let it begin with Ed Shipman.

It's amazing and necessary to the story to understand the scope of what Happy Hill began with, to understand the breadth of what it has become and to see the possibilities for all of the rest. Located an hour-and-a-half southeast of Dallas, it has accomplished so much in a very unique way.

All of the other homes throughout this country have either been created by people hundreds of years ago who drew upon large wealth, or more recently by large institutions whose missions matched the purpose of an orphanage. That makes perfect sense.

Children's homes, then and even more so now, are expensive, time-consuming, controversial, heavily regulated propositions that are in constant need of more money, more effort, and for the children, a kind of love that is generally reserved for family, because for these children, it is family.

They are a venture that, once drawn into, can be near impossible to get out of because the march of children in need never ends. No wonder so few take on the task so directly, while most of the rest of us are unaware the homes are even there.

But in 1975 Ed, along with his wife, Gloria, looked at the problem of so many children with nowhere to go and instead saw opportunity.

However, at first, Ed and Gloria had completely different plans. Now married for fifty-two years, they met in South Carolina and moved to Fort Worth so that Ed could graduate from seminary.

Ed first spent years working in newspaper advertising and then radio and TV public relations before starting a foundation in Fort Worth where his job was land development while spending every weekend as a pastor tending to rural communities. The course of his life seemed to be set—he was in his early forties, had a comfortable lifestyle, a good marriage, two healthy sons, Todd who was fourteen and Chuck who was twelve, and they were all getting the chance to enjoy some of the fruits of his labor.

A lot of us can appreciate where his life had gotten to; we dream of riches, whether we ever manage to accumulate anything or not. It's the reason the lottery is so popular. But fortunately, there are some who build a dream knowing riches will never be a part of the grand plan. Everything they managed to do for others only truly becomes apparent, the grand plan at last revealed, when they retire or at their funeral, when all of the lives they touched show up to pay homage. It's only as the pieces come together in the sea of faces gathered to celebrate the human being that everyone gets a clear view of the envisioned dream and how well it has all come to pass.

Ed Shipman is that kind of man. He's in the thirty-second year of an unexpected passion, finally getting to the place where others share his zeal and help out more easily. The Dallas Cowboys pitch in for an annual luncheon and cookbook fundraiser, and CEOs of large corporations donate money every year to the home.

But they still don't see how far out it all stretches, how far he's come, how much he's still driven to press farther into the edges of his dreams.

Back in 1975 Ed was a family man earning a good living in construction. "I had a very fine life; had all the stuff that comes with that lifestyle," he said, with no plans to change anything. He would coast for a while, finish raising the two teenage boys, plan for a nice retirement. A nice life, all in all.

There's something in Ed, though, that made what happened inevitable. An essential ingredient for anyone who suddenly takes a sharp turn in middle age that has nothing to do with the cliché of a mid-life crisis.

Ed always made a point of listening to the small inner voice that a lot of us are very good at drowning out. Ed not only listened, he followed through with conviction, sure of something larger than himself, willing to step out there, trusting in the end results.

So, when the turning point came, when the marshal called to say they had two teenage girls, sisters, who needed a place to stay until the authorities could find them a bed somewhere, Ed and Gloria took a good look at the girls and felt some parental responsibility. The same kind any parent feels if they hear a child yell out, "Mom!" or "Dad!" in a store. We all turn to look, the innate connection we share, making sure help is there, everything is all right, before we turn back to the sweater we were eyeing.

They listened to the inner voice and took the girls in with the inner understanding that they'd help find the needed beds. They offered the girls a safe, clean place to stay while sorting out where the sisters belonged, what the next step would be to repair or create a life. The Shipmans traveled the state of Texas visiting different children's homes, looking for two beds. Eventually, they found a place for them at the Round Rock Children's Baptist Home in Austin.

But along the way, what they also saw was the rising tide of children who needed a whole-life program, a place to grow up and learn life-skills, and the more they looked the more they saw those faces, those of other misplaced children with nowhere to go. Without a glance backward Ed and Gloria's old life unraveled and a new one came together.

Here is the exact spot where most of us start tallying up what we have to lose—the cool possessions we've gathered—and the responsibilities we have to gauge—children, spouse—and we understand we won't be going another step further. We lament our shortcomings and the dire circumstances of some people, other people than ourselves, but we let go of the problem and return to the familiar and the comfortable. It was all we could do, we'll say at the next neighborhood party, recounting how tragic the whole thing was and how someone, a politician or social worker, should do something.

Even Ed had those thoughts, spending months talking over what to do with his family and friends and praying for guidance, even though he knew he'd already been given everything he needed to know.

Move forward, trust in the grand plan and hold on tight. Ed went for it.

"I had a faith, no voices from the sky, but some great feeling that I was committed to a task I was destined to do. When that happens, you just keep doing it," he said.

"I got sympathy from my peer group," said Ed, chuckling in a distinct Texas drawl mixed in with his South Carolina roots. "They thought I was nuts. I had more fun with that than anything else."

When Ed first saw the land, back when he worked as a developer for the foundation, it was a forest of scrub and pine, typical Texas landscape, with a small tilled area in the front used for farming. An old house, a hundred years old, sat near the main road and was occupied till the land was sold. In 1973 Ed had brush cleared on half of the property and cut a road to the top.

Ed bought the land with plans to build houses and laid out plats, selling fourteen or fifteen tracts, four of the spec homes went to friends, when change found him.

First things first, Ed went around to each of the families now living on the land, the Browns—family friends—included, and explained what he planned to do with the rest of the property. He explained his change in direction and that a residential education facility was going to spring up around them and that he understood if they had reservations about sticking around. Ed offered to buy back the homes at the fair market value to allow anyone who wanted to move someplace else. Ed has always been about doing what's right, without worry about lack or means.

It's how the Happy Hill Farm still operates, without any debt of any kind. No state or federal money is accepted and less than 10 percent of the annual budget comes from fees paid by parents or family members. The bulk of the money comes from private donations from corporations, non-profits, and individuals. All of the children are privately placed, which means no children from Social Services. However, social workers have been known to recommend the farm to families who are in crisis, before a child has to be removed by the authorities. Divorced parents have to come to an understanding that the child will remain on campus year-round like all of the other children, coming home for holidays and breaks. In the thirty-two years the Farm has been in operation only thirty kids have attempted to run away, which was unnecessary. Asking to go would have been enough. No child has to stay, and every child has to show a willingness to be there in the first place.

"During orientation, we will say, 'you're an invited guest. If you ever get to the point when you're so depressed, you want to run away, come to one of us and we will put you in the car and drive you home,'" said Ed.

Linda, a petite ninth grader with long dark hair, steps in front of me in the dining hall and fixes me with a searching look. "Has my brother been talking about me?" she asks. Her brother, Richard, a seventh grader, has been telling a lot of stories, none about Linda. As a matter of fact, he made a point of saying he wasn't going to tell me anything about her. He'd been warned, he said, smiling with a grin that seems to imply he knows plenty. I didn't tempt him by asking too many questions.

Linda is leaving the Farm for another residential education facility with fewer rules. She has been at the Farm for four years and will be heading to a Methodist home in Waco where she's convinced fewer rules will be more fun. It's a tricky balance, rules versus freedom, when to let go of a rule and when to hold fast. Most parents know that and every home I visit constantly reviews policy, listens to kids, teachers, counselors, searching for the fluid resting spot.

There is no dancing at the Farm, not a lot of secular movies or music or video games, and the dress code requires girls' hemlines to be at least as long as the end of their fingertips. There's no cleavage, no midriffs, and shorts are worn under skirts and dresses. An incident some years back with a troubled girl who was prone to flashing led to the last rule.

Dating is a privilege for the older kids and is chaperoned at an adult cottage with a strict "six inch rule" that means everybody keeps at least six inches apart from each other. Cheryl Kavathas, Ed's very efficient assistant who was an event planner in Dallas before she started at the Farm nine years ago with the intention of staying a few months and now lives on campus, pointed out, "Thirty-two years and no pregnancy."

The prom is a Texas dress-up affair but bears more of a resemblance to a coffee house with Christian-themed music. Ed is actually the only one who refers to the event as a "prom." However, the formal nights—prom and the sports awards banquet—are both taken very seriously.

A just-us-girls shopping trip heads out to the nearby big city of Dallas to find fancy formal dresses for the awards banquet and all of the girls are thrilled to be heading to the mall. Jasmine is from New Orleans and wants to some day be president and have a very large staff. Ronda will be graduating and heading on to Texas A&M to learn international business. Katie is the furthest away, her family is back in San Diego, and Liz is from nearby Garland and is thinking about becoming a nurse.

The dresses fly by in shades of deep aqua blue or a dark copper and shoes are contemplated, as are purses. Each girl has to come out and model the dress, partly so we can go on a little about the beautiful girl wearing the dress and also so it can be checked to make sure it's within the dress code's parameters. All of them are.

The constant running back and forth between the shoe department and the dresses wears me out. During one quick trip back to match shoes we run into Sherrie Ivey, a social worker at the Farm who is buying shoes for herself. The girls gather around for hugs and a quick consultation. Sherrie used to be with Child Protective Services in nearby Fort Worth but has found more satisfaction at the Farm where she can openly discuss her faith and use that foundation as another tool. She also has the opportunity to watch the kids, like these girls, grow up, graduate, get married, and build lives of their own. A full circle. "That part's really special. My most special memory was in 1997 when five kids I had started with when they were in the seventh grade, watching them graduate," she said.

The girls are happy to see her and slow down, just for a moment, to sit next to her and glance through the small tower of boxes she has accumulated, humming about their day. It is a tableau that bears a strong resemblance to the favorite aunt surrounded by a gaggle of nieces.

Soon we are on the move again, snaking back through the racks to the dresses completely focused on the mission. I sit in a chair by the dressing room watching the ritual that helps move a young girl closer to adulthood—shopping with intent. Quickly, I become the guardian of the purses as they draw together in small clusters to decide which shade of blue is better or whether or not there are shoes to go with the dress, and if there aren't shoes, to start hunting through the racks again. There is no arguing, no whispering from one girl to the next, no rolling of the eyes throughout the entire trip. They are more confident than most of my middle-aged friends.

One girl hangs back and has to be coaxed into trying something on; she doesn't have enough money to afford a dress in this fancy Dallas mall. Janel Dunn, who is one of their house parents, quietly pays for the dress that had the most consensus and surprises the girl, who gives a small smile of relief. Everyone has something new to wear to the big banquet.

We all head to the food court to hang out and people-watch. I ask one of the girls if she's glad to be at the Farm. "Yes," she replies.

"Why?"

"Because if I wasn't here I'd probably be in jail."

She says it so matter-of-factly; her pale blue eyes looking straight into mine lack any judgment about her pronouncement. It's a fact she has come to realize: Happy Hill Farm gave her a shot at another kind of life and she has taken it. College awaits her next year.

Back at the farm, Ed and I are taking another turn around the grounds as he points out where everything began. He has just as much energy as the girls on their shopping trip. I'm grateful we're driving up and down the winding roads and not walking.

Up on the hill where there is the best view of what a dream can

The campus in the winter.

become, there is a house with sweeping front windows where Scotty and Sylvia Brown still live, the hold-outs when everyone else moved out. Everyone who had bought a home back in 1975 took Ed up on the buy-back offer with this one notable exception.

The Browns decided to stay and went one step further. They opened their home to the Shipman family and the first residents of the farm, two boys who had managed to get kicked out of every school they had ever attended. That's right, everyone moved in with the Browns.

The Browns' front room, which has a sweeping view of the campus, was the chapel on Sunday mornings, and the dining room became the dining hall. Four adults and four children crammed into one ranch-style house with two of the kids working out serious behavioral issues.

Sylvia Brown, still neat and trim with brown hair, gives a patient smile and insists that there were no heated discussions, no arguments over territory or a lot of long walks as people looked for a little space. Ed and Gloria are seated next to them at a table with the same serene smile, nodding in agreement. No power struggles; no one feeling the need to define their personal boundaries. It's like they're the antithesis of talk show guests, already comfortable in their own skin long before the gestation of the farm. Ed says that the need for control, the need to know how or why or when, was surrendered to God a long time ago and he lives in the moment with gratitude. I've heard plenty of people say that, and at some point stake a claim to something and get a little territorial. I've come to expect it and understand: there's the soft underbelly of the person. The area they're still working to surrender. The only time Ed truly seems uncomfortable is when the light is turned on him and people want to tell him how wonderful he is. He waves his hand and says some version of "Oh, come on," but even then, no arguments. He lets it be.

I dutifully take all of it down but how to get to where he's standing is eluding me. How to become the kind of parent Louie needs and find some measure of peace or general sense of sanity. Mostly, I keep remembering how easy it was to make Louie happy when he was small and how impossible it is now, and I wonder when exactly everything changed. The boundary I felt between the parents of all of the children at any of the homes and myself was so clear when I took on this project. I was on one side, the side with those who could figure enough of it out, and on the other were the parents of hundreds of thousands of children who have to learn a new definition of home and family. The "just couldn't figure it out, maybe didn't try hard enough" side. Suddenly the boundary was getting a little fuzzy and I wasn't sure where I stood or what to do.

We stopped in a popular restaurant in town, Stringfellows, and the owner, Diane Davis, is an old friend of the Shipmans. Her affection for them is genuine and obvious and her niece and nephew are growing up at the farm. She has an easy smile and tells me that when she was younger her mother used to use the farm as a threat to keep the kids in line. Happy Hill Farm was the bogeyman. The hold of the *Annie* myth is strong no matter where I am, or what kind of home it is—no matter what term is used to describe the home: orphanage or residential education facility or academy; no matter the success stories or success rate of the people who have lived here. The news doesn't seem to get out far beyond the walls to where it could be useful for a lot of other people.

Back at the Farm, standing on the road up behind the row of cottages, back on the hills again, I can see most of the campus laid out below, and it looks more like a village. There is a real sense of community among all of the residents, which includes a lot of the staff who live on the grounds. Two boys, both seniors, go running by us, waving to Mr. Shipman as they stop for a moment to tell him how graduation plans are coming. Both have been accepted into colleges in Texas and appear confident and self-assured. They start back down the road, running easily as the adult who started out with them finally catches up, giving a slightly worn-out smile as he keeps chugging along behind the boys.

A girls' basketball game in the Happy Hill gym.

Ed chuckles and gives a brief run-down of the boys' histories, which includes the standard litany of falling behind and losing direction. What's amazing is to witness the end result. The two young men were not only looking me in the eye while I spoke and addressing me as ma'am, they were able to reel off their plans after the Farm and they did it with confidence. They expect everything to work out okay. It's an Ed trait.

There is a gym off to the left of where I'm standing, with a pool and tennis courts. Next to that is a fine arts center with a recording center and a woodworking shop nearby. Clyde Crittenden is an older gentleman who helped develop the woodworking program and has been volunteering for the past fourteen years. A lot of troubled boys have sat next to him working on a bird house or spice rack, spending two or three hours at a time quietly working on some old hurt feelings.

Most of the buildings were designed by Gloria Shipman who would find a building she liked somewhere else and use the aspects she liked to design each building on the farm. "A lot of the limestone used in the newer buildings came from here on the farm," said Ed.

Near the school is a barber shop with the requisite pole and the only old buildings still standing from when the Happy Hill Farm began, including three old barracks buildings Ed bought for $300 and the donated little red school house complete with steeple. The farm has its own water system and waste treatment and takes care of its own roads. "We've worn out a couple of dump trucks, tractors, years ago," said Ed. A big Caterpillar dealer in Dallas lent the first tractors to clear the land.

To the right, halfway up from the road, is a stocked lake, and a teacher in a straw hat is taking a little time off to fish with his young son. The lake is stocked with big bass, catfish, and sun perch and relies on a 'put-back' policy.

"If you catch one, you can admire it," says Ed, "and then you put it back."

The state-of-the-art agricultural center built in 1999 is down near the gym. It was an easy pitch to Texas donors who see raising animals as a rite of passage. Most of the children twelve and above are in 4H and keep an animal. The little ones start with a goat or a lamb, moving their way up to a pig and then ultimately, when they're in high school, the care of a steer or heifer. The animals are all entered into competitions and any monies received are put into personal college funds. Sometimes the money can be substantial.

All of the meat consumed on the farm comes from animals raised there. It's always been the case, particularly in the early days when money was tight. For the first three years of the Happy Hill's existence everything that was consumed there was raised there, plant or animal, and anything that could be preserved to last through the year, was put into jars or frozen.

Sylvia and Scotty go walking by, as they do every evening, side by side, and are now a permanent part of the Farm family. Now, there's a real dining hall fondly referred to as Sylvia's kitchen. All of the kids eat lunch and dinner in the dining hall; breakfast is in the individual cottages.

Girls and boys eat at separate times in the dining hall. They had been eating together, but there was a lot of carrying-on and not a lot of eating. The rule was changed.

Today, a church group from Possum Kingdom Lake, which they explain is west of here and not near anything, is visiting the home and we're all having lunch together in the dining hall. People on the tour who've been there before keep wondering out loud if they'll be lucky enough to get some of Sylvia's famous cookies.

The church regularly donates to the home and occasionally takes field trips to see what their money has helped to create. It's like a mission trip in reverse. Groups of people come to the Farm to be reminded of what's possible, if only to let go of what they were taught. Let go of the old idea that constructing anything, particularly something outside of what we're used to, what our family has done before, is next to impossible, prone to failure, and painful. Best not try. To let go of that.

Everyone here knows Ed and knows better than to bring the complaints with them, and that leaves room for listening, and this is part of the peculiar magic of Ed Shipman. If I can't voice my fears, my worries, or complaints and instead have to steer my thoughts in a new direction, I can start to hear things I was missing before. I can start to let ideas grow into a possibility, rather than stepping on them right away.

If you want to test this one out for yourself among your own peers, start lobbing the germ of a good idea you've been carrying around and pay attention to what kind of feedback you get. Is it how to make it bigger or warnings about what could go wrong? I started to notice how often people said, "The problem with that is ..." and how that was viewed as helpful. I also started to notice the absence of it on the farm. Not only an absence but how often others were chiming in with how to build the germ into something substantial. People offered names, numbers. It happened consistently and carried with it the power of potential.

The church group is chatty and charming and says hello to children they recognize from previous trips. Cookies appear and they let out grateful sounds of "ooohs" for the Sylvia trademark. Cheryl is acting as hostess, fetching more coffee as Ed tries to answer any questions.

Scotty now takes care of much of the grounds, and, besides the dining hall, Sylvia makes sure each of the cottages is as neat as a pin.

After he had worked out the care and feeding with the Browns and his family, Ed's next immediate concern in 1975 was how to educate the two boys who had been entrusted to his care. None of the local schools would take them in, citing their records, so Ed traveled to the Texas state capitol in Austin and asked for help. They handed him a manual and wished him well.

This is where Ed's penchant for running with the nearest good idea has served him well. He didn't lament the turn of events or worry about which path to take. He just moved forward. Someone donated that little red schoolhouse, complete with a small steeple, which they had moved to the property, and others donated books and the needed materials. Ed spoke to teachers he wanted to hire and made them a promise.

Although he couldn't afford to pay them right away, he'd keep them fed and their gas tanks full and pay every cent he owed them as soon as he was able. Ed kept his word and a year later each teacher received a large check for every penny they were owed. Several of them still say it wasn't a bad way to get paid and made their salary seem a lot bigger. The principal, and several of the other administrators, moved on campus into some of the homes vacated by the families who had sold back their property.

Ed quit his job with the foundation in Fort Worth to give the new path his full attention, to make a commitment, and figured out he had enough money to last for one year. He started small with a licensed group foster home that quickly grew into a residential facility that he ran out of a trailer.

"The immediate community thought we were bringing a lot of juvenile delinquents and putting them in the middle of their community."

Ed worked hard to sway people over to his way of thinking, raising $30,000 the first year while he established his credibility with both those inside the profession and out.

But not everyone was willing to listen. In 1976, one year after they had begun, the County Commissioners of Hood County, a group of fifteen men, insisted the Farm had to pay taxes, even as a non-profit. Ed had heard the rumblings all over town and knew the real motive was a cowardly attempt to shut Happy Hill down to stop the influx of black children. Many had used the derogatory "n-word" when mentioning some of the children who were getting a fresh start.

Ed Shipman would have none of it and fought the county commissioners in court, winning the case. The county appealed to the State of Texas Supreme Court and lost again, and only then did they relent. Change was allowed in the door. It was coming anyway.

Fundraising, though, was going to prove to be more of a lesson. "There are disappointments and places you get stone walled," said Ed, explaining how he felt those first few years when he had more expectations than results.

At first, he had assumed that all of the various religious groups he knew, had been affiliated with, and had built a strong bond with, would automatically donate to the cause. He thought they'd understand what he was doing without a lot of explanation or flying the flag of any particular denomination.

"I wanted to stay out of denominations even though I knew that would handicap us," said Ed, "but I did expect some of the people that I knew who were members of churches to understand what para-denominational was, like Billy Graham. I expected churches to quickly understand and help if even modestly."

Ed is driving along the roads of the home again, pointing out the

A group of students at the stables.

new projects as he remembers those early days. There's no anxiety creeping up in his voice, no tinges of resentment. It's just a part of the story, part of the learning curve in his walk of faith.

"We were in this for a year and I started looking at the whole thing and realized if something didn't change, in five years we would be the same and die on the vine so I went to any place I could think of that wasn't a church. Kiwanis, Rotarians, Chamber of Commerce. Around that second and third year we started growing."

And Ed's penchant for believing in the possibilities without first weighing the why-nots really paid off again. In 1977 Happy Hill was planning a country and western concert with a motorcycle club as a fundraiser. Jeannie Riley, the singer famous for the song, "Harper Valley PTA," was the headliner.

Somebody threw out the idea that getting a Dallas Cowboy football player to attend would help fill the place. Ed heard a good idea, didn't ask anyone's opinion, it just wasn't in his nature, and dialed the main number of the Cowboys. He explained why he was calling and somehow, they listened, even mulled over the request, offering up a young player, Bob Bruenig, as a possible candidate. Bruenig agreed, and once the media found out, the night of the fundraiser the Tarrytown Arena was filled with paying customers. A new era for Happy Hill had begun.

In 1980 Tom Landry joined the board, and a Cowboys' cookbook was put together. Each year, there's an annual Dallas Cowboy luncheon where many corporations trade in-kind with food or uniforms for the farm in exchange for tables and a chance to meet Cowboy football players. The farm's credibility grew.

Even now, Ed doesn't mention what might have gone wrong, what could have happened. It's only in the absence of all of that chatter that I realize how much so many of us operate our lives based on managing against failure. The fact that almost all of it never does happen and we held ourselves back from trying as a consequence had never really occurred to me before.

It's like I've been trying to hold back unseen disasters for years, and now, with Louie, I'm failing miserably anyway. All of my efforts were pointless. I wonder for a moment what that says about my judgment, my abilities, my choices.

Ed points out that throughout the home's long history there have still been economic pitfalls and doomsayers. But none of that is the point. The place to stay focused is on the end results, the vision, and knowing the answers will be provided.

I've never operated like that and I'm not sure I have it in me to let go.

Up the highway from the farm there are eighty-one acres Happy Hill wants to use and the county commissioners are again denying the tax exemption. "Son of a gun, here we go again," said Ed, shaking his head. "You don't do this without somebody who's negative." He shrugs his shoulders and goes back to pointing out where the new inn will be that will accommodate thirty-five visitors overnight, or the stadium and track that will cost a million dollars. How the dispute will be resolved is not up to Ed Shipman, it's up to a Higher Power. He lets it all go and points out another new feature.

Like most big ideas, the proof of whether or not it was ever a good idea is in hindsight. Today, Happy Hill Farm Academy has an on-site fully accredited K-12 school on 260 of the 500 acres of a working farm with enough beds for 110 children in a dozen cottages. Children are placed in the cottages based on age and behavior and can earn points based on a behavior modification system, which can allow children to move on to a different cottage with more privileges or back, if points are lost. The new school for seventh to twelfth grade has 60,000 square feet and contains two new computer labs with bigger classrooms and a family and consumer center with ovens and sewing machines. The new library is three times bigger than the center with skylights to let in natural light.

At the doors of the school is a metal detector, required by law, that has become very useful at picking up on the foil wrappers around gum, but fortunately has not discovered anything more nefarious.

The total annual budget of the farm is five million dollars. Each child's care costs around $30,000 with the private school being the most expensive component. However, this is minimal compared to the $60,000 per year price tag for locking up a youth in Texas, that doesn't include what the child might have contributed to a community as an adult who believed in their own dreams, their own potential.

Dru Pruitt, the principal at the school, is in her seventh year of watching children grow from anger, fear, and doubt about ever having any kind of future to confidently stepping out into the world beyond the farm.

Justin has become one of those kids. He was a junior in high school when we met, had been at the farm for four years and initially stood out as a troublemaker from the day he entered the doors of the school.

"An act of God brought me here," he says, smiling. "At my old school I didn't fit in, my mom and I had grown apart. I'd slipped into depression." He recounts the early days with no self-possession, no attachment to who he used to be. "It was hard the first couple of months. I was loud, obnoxious, the class clown. I spent a lot of time in detention."

Justin's behavior got him short-listed on Chuck Shipman's *List of Kids*. Chuck now oversees the day-to-day operations of the farm and keeps a running list of kids who may not be staying due to behavioral issues. An emergency family conference was called with Justin's mom, Justin, his teachers, counselors, and Dru in attendance. Justin's grades weren't part of the problem at this point.

While he had tested most of the rules (including who would blink first on issues of homework) and had been sent back a level in his cottage, due to the small classes with a ratio of four students to every teacher he was still getting As and Bs. It was his determination to not fit in, not listen, not work with anyone that had landed him on *the list*.

At the conference he gave more of the same, saying he didn't want to be there, and he didn't care what anyone thought. A standard outer shell for a child who's tired of being let down by others and has decided to go first by pushing everyone else for the foreseeable future.

But Justin was given the opportunity to hear what Dru and the other teachers thought of him and his potential and what they were willing to do to help him. He heard a different message. Even though he had pushed them, pushed hard, they were on his side and they believed he could do the work. Love with accountability.

Dru breaks in to the conversation. "Every time I saw Justin in the hall I'd say, 'Justin, be quiet,' and every time he'd argue with me. The first parent/teacher conference his mom kept hushing him," she says in a soft Texas drawl.

"Before I was such an act," said Justin, "had to act loud, act bad. I got to know myself here."

His most memorable moment was when he managed to receive a detention in Ms. Shaw's class that read "not coming out of the closet," for stubbornly refusing to get out of the closet. It had started as a prank and grown into a small act of will. But now, looking back, they are cracking up remembering how the slight teenager stood his ground and took his detention.

"There was a transition through the ninth grade," said Dru. "Every time he did something right, we let him know that positive. We mainly want kids to know we care about them *and* it's our way," she added.

And then, the summer before his sophomore year, Ed, or Mr. Shipman as all of the kids call him, took Justin aside. "He took time to talk to me," said Justin, "and said forget about the past. You have so much in front of you." He tears up, apologizing, and wiping his eyes on his sleeve.

A gradual change overtook him then that was mostly noticed in hindsight.

Dru had her own rite of passage to go through when she arrived at Happy Hill. "It was hard at first because when I taught third grade everyone loved me: the parents, the kids. I came here and was the disciplinarian and I would go to a basketball game and no one would sit next to me. Took four years."

An adjustment was needed that had to come from the inside, out. "I was used to telling a third grader to sit down and do their work. I'd tell a kid here and they'd argue and I'd argue back. I'd raise my voice. At first, I got my feelings hurt a lot."

Her move to the farm had happened quickly. The former principal was already gone when Dru arrived and with two weeks notice at her old school, she changed jobs, moved on campus, and learned on the job how to deal with the newer kids who came in with a chip on their shoulder.

It took a while, but veterans of the farm kept gently telling her not to take anything personally, not to argue back, and to calmly stand her ground. Eventually, the message got through. This wasn't a contest of wills and Dru had nothing to prove.

The goal of Happy Hill is to let each child know they can do the work, they're expected to do the work, and the best they can do is all that's being asked of them. No contests there either.

If a child fails to turn in an assignment they get to sit with Dru every afternoon till it's done. No games, no TV, no socializing. When they come for the admissions interview Dru tells them, they will do the work. However, that doesn't stop many children from testing the limits, particularly if they're used to a system that would rather pass over them than wait them out.

"The longest it ever took one boy to do an assignment was two weeks," said Dru, smiling because she knows the end to the story. It's the same ending for every child at a place where no one can fail. "He finally said, 'You're not going to give up, are you?' and he wrote the most beautiful essay in 45 minutes."

This is the turning point for most children who pass through the doors of any of these modern children's homes. They finally hit that place where adults on the outside have thrown up their hands in a "it's your life" kind of gesture and *allowed* them to fail. All of us have that place where we find it difficult to push beyond. For some children, some people, the bar is set low and the expectations are very limited. These are the children, for the most part, who show up at these homes.

The farm's "no fail" policy is the reason children who are used to running the show, getting into trouble, and following their own set of fluid internal rules will listen to Ed, an evangelical ordained minister who doesn't allow dancing or alcohol to even be on the premises, and very limited dating. They know they've finally met someone who believes, without reservation, that all things are possible, that they have a rightful place in this world, and that Ed Shipman loves them, just as they are.

That's key. Growing up at a seminary gave me the opportunity to observe the "men of God" who felt it necessary to occasionally needle someone about their past, perhaps as a way to make sure they were minding their ps and qs in the present. But, all it ever did was give someone the opportunity to drag the weight of everything they judged about themselves behind them, fill them with fear about what else they might do to add to the baggage, and make them take fewer risks of any kind. And life is all about change, which means risk.

Susan Blair, a social worker at Happy Hill and the girls' counselor for college and careers, is responsible for helping the girls manage most of the changes that are to come, as well as the transformations they will need to make in the day-to-day living that keeps occurring in life.

"We go over various possible scenarios for college to inoculate against failure. I try to lead them through the thinking process of SAT scores, expensive versus inexpensive schools, or [schools] close to home. We have to first match reality, then we can match emotion."

This is the same theme that carries through every home: deal with what is, take responsibility, and believe in what can become. No running away from anything, but there is the need to move on from what no longer works. No mental hanging-on to the past.

That can come into play sometimes with visits home to old neighborhoods, old routines.

Children come to the farm often with no sense of boundaries, for both what is expected of them and what they can reasonably expect of others. After awhile, trust is built up to the point where it becomes easier to listen and rules start to make sense. It becomes less about who has the power and more about a set of goals that are agreed upon by the children and the adults in their life.

The larger goal is to have a child achieve maturity, leave the farm, and still be setting personal goals, sometimes in concert with a spouse or a boss, while understanding which rules reasonably apply and recognizing when it's time to leave or change.

However, sometimes children grow up at the Farm, learning how to work toward a goal, trust, and listen to their own intuition, while the home life has remained the same. Visits home become an opportunity, says Susan Blair, to stay up all night, play on-line, and slip back into destructive patterns. It can be tough to re-integrate.

"Parenting on the extremes is bad in both directions. Abuse has horrible outcomes but parenting with no backbone produces self-centered adults. We want to help children feel good or satisfied about who they are," said Blair.

"The communication with parents is constant. Parent/teacher conferences occur every six or seven weeks. Every family gets a calendar for the year with the dates on it and they know about it a week before. We send out a reminder letter to those within driving distance."

For those adults who are willing, Susan will work on basic parenting skills, such as how to give reasonable consequences that fit the age and how to develop good communication skills. Consistency and communication are key to building a good relationship with all of the family

The garden in summer.

members. "We just have so many kids with all sorts of families and it works for everybody," she said.

Back on the hillside standing next to Ed and looking down at the small village, it is possible for me to see what can happen if I can push through the moments when all there is, is a belief or desire. The places where it may only be me and a conviction in something bigger guiding me along. That's what I've learned from Ed; that it's not the province of only a few, but of everyone, including Louie and me, if we can hold fast. It's all a matter of perspective. I can turn around and see the acreage that is overgrown and tangled, difficult to maneuver. Or, I can choose to look down the hill at the possibilities.

For Ed the dream is realized and he is congratulated as a visionary. His two grown sons work at Happy Hill by his side with their wives. Over 80 percent of the kids from the farm go on to college and all of the funds, over $5 million annually, come from private sources.

But, Ed's still leaning hard on his faith and hears that voice to keep growing—at seventy he's just not done yet. There are plans to start building more cottages soon and Ed has been appearing on national talk shows to raise awareness about the need for more places just like his—not fewer as some advocates hope. He has been taking in children from outside the Dallas area who have heard about the success stories of the children raised at Happy Hill and there's a waiting list that grows longer every week. Ed made an appearance on the popular daytime TV talk show *Dr. Phil*, who's a fellow Texan, and received over 5,000 phone calls from interested people.

Now, the farm is in the middle of a fifteen-year expansion that has begun with a medical clinic that will have two young pediatricians from Houston who will serve not only the farm but also local kids who are without the means to receive care elsewhere. There is new construction everywhere. Across the small road near the gated entrance is the beginning of a new welcome center that will include a coffee bar and video presentation of the history of the farm. A memorial garden is slated for nearby. Ed's vision is expanding.

"We're in the first stage of an expansion," he says, "the new academic facility starts construction in November [2006]. We're going to build a small stadium for football. We have a nice gym, tennis courts, a pool. I want to build a larger theater for drama—we have a recording studio," he says, quickly taking a breath before diving back into the list. He can see all of it, already there.

There is something called "a walk of faith" that simply translated means leaving every how and why up to a higher power, believing that all things will be handled in time and forgiveness sincerely asked for is instantly granted.

Without ever stating it, Ed is walking that path without faltering and has gathered around him a staff that is endeavoring to do the same. I know that few will believe it's possible for someone, anyone, to go through life without worrying about how things might go wrong. I'm not sure I could have believed it without seeing it for myself. Maybe Ed Shipman is someone that has to be witnessed to be believed, or maybe that's faith too. I know that I was blessed to have found myself as his guest for awhile and seen the challenges he faces.

I was going to need it when I flew home to Louie.

~∞~

My son had occasionally answered the phone, said hello before saying he had to go, or just hung up. I left a string of messages and felt ridiculous witnessing transformations of other children, knowing my own was slipping from my grasp. Friends would have explained it away as the necessary separation a teenager takes from their parents but I knew something else was up and it was far darker.

When I got home from Texas, it was late and the house was dark. Louie was nowhere to be found and everything was in a shambles. The carpet in the center of the living room had a large damp brown circle and reeked of beer. All of the furniture on the first floor had been moved and hastily put back in a similar position. Someone had taken a key to the chair railing around the dining room and chipped away at it all the way around the room. Deliberate, angry digs that exposed the pine underneath. The kitchen timer was broken, dishes were scattered everywhere. Someone had ransacked the freezer and spilled a bag of frozen peas, leaving them spread across the freezer and the floor. An old, sparkly lip gloss was in the upstairs bathroom and a girl's halter top was left behind. Bits and pieces of someone else's clothes—a sock, a shirt, a towel, a bathing suit—were scattered here and there. Louie was nowhere to be seen.

He hadn't been to school the entire time I had been gone, missing days he couldn't afford in his senior year of high school. There was an email from his advocate at school marked as urgent that said Louie had fallen behind and wasn't turning in assignments. He might not graduate. All of the lies I had been telling myself were failing me.

An enormous weight centered itself in the middle of my chest and stayed there, weighing me down. It became impossible to move, and I didn't attempt to fix anything, leaving everything right where it was, letting go of it all.

Everything I had ever dreamed of stopped for a moment and held still, momentarily destroyed by this one idea: I had failed as a mother, and I had profoundly failed Louie.

A small memory of a different Louie came back to me as I sat on the couch in the dark living room. We were coming out of the grocery store near our house, and he was just three years old.

"Can we sit down for a few minutes?" asked Louie. "I want to watch everybody." He smiled up at me and waited for my answer. To do that, I had to set down the bags and put us somewhat in the way of all of those quick-moving feet trying to get something done.

I looked down at his face, ready to say no, knowing it was the expected answer I was supposed to give.

"Sure," I said, surprising only me. I felt a rush of wind inside of myself. It's the only way I can describe it. The feeling of a strong wind momentarily blowing through me. There was an actual hole in the fear I usually carried around and I felt a small piece of joy unattached to anything in particular.

Louie and I sat down, balanced on the edge of the grimy curb as people said, "excuse me," all around us, some more politely than others.

"Martha," a surprised neighbor said, "do you need a ride home? Did the car break down?"

"We're fine," I said. "We're taking a break."

Louie looked up at me and smiled, and went back to watching the people come and go. So, this is joy, I thought, breathing in deeply. We sat there for an hour.

I tried Louie's number with no answer. He's ignoring me again, but it's not the typical teenager-pulling-away treatment. He has pulled away and is working at self-destructing. Rolls of memories go by me while I sit in the dark.

Birthday parties in elementary school that involved his entire class. One year we visited a beekeeper. Another year everyone dressed as pirates and we marched through our neighborhood on a quest for the pieces of a map. Neighbors dressed up and played parts until the kids eventually found the treasure of chocolate coins. Or the afternoons spent watching football, t-ball, basketball, lacrosse, or soccer practices. Then there were the vacations to the beach and rides on the Ocean City, New Jersey, boardwalk and the trips to the playground or the park or to see the fireworks or visit Santa. A life I thought we had passed before me, and I was forced to finally let go of any pretenses; but still I searched for anything I may have done right so that I could survive what is the new reality.

There is such anger in this home now. Anger made visible and even in the silence it is so real I couldn't think of anything but I tried desperately to figure out if I could have prevented any of it. Did I cause all of it, and, if I did, when did we take that wrong turn that had to lead to here? I felt compelled to take a deep breath and search for whatever remained, even if it's just the memories of some other time—like when he was small and I still thought he was full of a magic I couldn't destroy and might even learn something from.

"He looks like one of the Blue Men, you know, from the Revolution." Leave it to Dad to come up with an historical reference and cite the American side. We are a family of descendants of famous people. Looking for a connection to something of merit is like second nature.

Louie was standing at the front door clad in only his Ninja Turtle underwear, completely covered in an aqua blue coating. He had figured out his big, fat sticks of chalk dissolved in puddles. I was impressed with his attention to detail; even his eyelids and the backs of his ears had been smeared with the blue paint.

I wasn't surprised that he was up to something. That was life with Louie. Thank goodness I knew he was smarter than I was. That's what made it possible to be writing at the computer and look out a window to see him on his small tricycle, legs out to the sides, whizzing down our very steep driveway, his curly hair straightened by the wind blowing past him, and not worry. Or I'd watch him attempt to pet every living creature, sometimes getting nipped by the geese down by the nearby lake, and not worry. Eventually the geese gave in and let him gently stroke their heads and chat with them. They would turn their heads slightly and look at him till he was done talking.

He did get nipped a little hard once by a garden snake and it made him mad, very mad. His three-year-old self whipped the snake into a half-knot, for which he felt instantly sorrowful and he came to get me to help untie the snake.

"What?" I asked, in the middle of vacuuming. "You did what?"

"I tied a snake in a knot and I need you to help me untie it," he said, calmly.

I turned off the vacuum, still looking at his calm expression, wondering if maybe he meant something else and I would find something else tied in a knot. Tied a snake in a knot?

There, on the front step, was a long black garden snake slowly, very slowly, untying itself from a very tight half-knot.

"Help it," Louie said.

"Why did you do it?" I asked.

"It bit me," he said, offering up his hand with a small red mark, no skin was broken. "Untie it," he repeated, looking back down at the snake, which was fortunately making progress.

"No, it's getting somewhere. We'll let the snake handle this one."

Louie wasn't completely satisfied and stayed to make sure before depositing the snake back in the grass. It didn't try to bite him again.

An incident like that might have been enough for other mothers to keep their child penned up inside where they could be more closely monitored. But I let Louie play in the front yard of our small neighborhood without me right next to him. Louie had been trying to break out of the house since he was two, sometimes successfully. I was worn out by the time he was three.

I didn't think his little hands at two-years-old could get the door open, but one day one set of our elderly neighbors, the Szparas, were showing me pictures they had recently taken and in one of them was Louie, smiling broadly, still in his pajamas, obviously outside without my knowledge. Then, our next-door neighbor, Murray, sometimes referred to as the king of the cul-de-sac by Mr. Szpara, came to my door with Louie in tow, when I thought he was in his room. Louie had quietly, stealthily snuck out, and gone next door to ask Murray if he could come out and play. I started dead-bolting the doors.

"We can't get out, she locked the doors," he said glumly to his Aunt Diana, who smiled broadly in return. She was Louie's favorite aunt because of her easy laugh and conspiratorial air. That's what clued Louie in.

"You know where the key is?" he said, hope returning. She refused to tell him, so he went back to scheming, which I'm fairly certain she encouraged. For months Louie would ask every guest who ventured into the house (and was then locked in), if they were ready to go, could he walk them to their car? He did this with no expression on his face, leaving them to think they were unwanted. I was constantly having to explain Louie was trying to get outside.

"It's not you, I promise," I would say.

Getting him inside, from the car to the house, was always a long process. Louie wouldn't give in for at least fifteen minutes, sometimes a half hour, every time we pulled in the driveway, even if it was late at night and he was exhausted. He was outside and he saw it as precious time, and he was going to stay out there even if he had to keep shaking his head to stay awake.

So, I had to do something to entice him inside faster.

The lake behind the house was filled with tree frogs and bullfrogs and cicadas and crickets. It's a very loud chorus in the warmer months that I found very comforting.

But I was tired and had groceries and Louie wouldn't budge, wanting to go exploring in the woods behind the house, which meant I had to stay outside because, knowing Louie, he'd find a hollow tree and get stuck in it in the minute it would take me to put the groceries down inside.

"Do you hear that?" I said, with a touch of fear on my face. I wasn't trying to make him apoplectic so I kept it to a minimum, but enough to draw concern.

"What?" said Louie, standing up straight and trying to discern a new sound over the loud hum.

"The frogs," I said with meaning, drawing out the word and adding maybe a little more fear to my face, before turning and running into the house. Louie ran quickly behind me.

Yea, I thought, finally, something I can use.

The next day Louie was at a sitter's while I worked at some odd job, probably catering, one of the many jobs I had while I figured out how to be a writer.

"The oddest thing happened today," said Judy, the sitter.

"What?" I said, having completely forgotten about my own cleverness.

"I was downstairs and heard Louie getting up from his nap and moving things around. When I went upstairs to check on him, he had stuffed his blanket under the door and locked it. I called to him through the door, but all he would say is, *frogs*. Do you know what that means?"

I said I had no idea.

Life with Louie meant he had a personal relationship with the real Santa Claus who came to the 6th Street Marketplace in downtown Richmond, entering via a fireplace chimney set up in the room, his legs dangling (I have no idea how they rigged it all, much less talked a senior citizen into doing it).

Louie brought long letters about how he knew Santa could help out the world and he'd hand them to Santa, who read them out loud over a small microphone. People always cried while Louie sat there beaming.

When he was four he kept asking everyone we saw on the walk from the car to the magical chimney if we were suddenly at the North Pole. He also loudly informed all the children in line at the local mall that they weren't seeing the real Santa, the real Santa was downtown.

Life with Louie meant he decided, at five, to climb yet another tree, the very tall pine right outside our front door, and didn't stop until he was above the roofline. Wisely, he decided to sit on a comfortable branch and wait patiently for me to come looking for him. In the meantime he would yell hello to any neighbors he saw who would turn round and round looking for him, before giving up and just yelling hello back in the general direction of his voice. See? Everyone knew Louie and knew it must be something, but in the end, it would also be okay. That was life with Louie, then. Scary, potentially dangerous, weird, funny, sad, touching, and always turned out okay. I was the reluctant listener, but I was slowly getting there.

I stood underneath the tall pine, directing him down as I tried to gauge where to stand so I could act as a human mattress if necessary.

"He will grow up in spite of me; he will grow up in spite of me," I repeated for the umpteenth time.

When he got to the ground he gave himself one good shake, looked up at me with a grin and said, "You should see the view from up there!" He quickly turned and took off running to look for something else to discover.

His adventures were always an odd complement to my own adventures as an undiscovered writer and a good reminder on the days I wanted to give up and do something *sensible*. Sure, that would look like the reasonable thing to do and would have made a lot of people feel more comfortable, but would have drained all of the fun out of life and taken away the possibilities that risk can bring. Besides, I wanted to see the view from there.

All of that felt like a distant echo then and part of some other life that had ended with an abrupt slam of a door. There was no turning around, no getting back what we had in this new place. The pain was so palpable I found it difficult to stand. I had lost the connections that have meant the most to me. First, my father and now my son.

I wasn't sure what to expect now. I had to let go or I was lost.

Chapter 4

Political Pressures

The story of the Bethesda Home for Boys, Savannah, Georgia, founded in 1740 by George Whitefield

GLAEN'S STORY

> *"Inaction breeds doubt and fear. Action breeds confidence and courage. If you want to conquer fear, do not sit home and think about it. Go out and get busy."*
>
> **Dale Carnegie**

Glaen Richards, pronounced "Glenn," is what the younger boys call an old-timer. He was at the home from 1939 to 1944 when it still had a dairy farm and is full of stories from another time.

"The Depression brought me to Bethesda, I and my two brothers came out there in '39. We were from Savannah and my father had died. My mother brought us to Rome, Georgia but it was too much for her.

"I didn't feel too good about it at the time. You just find a niche that you feel comfortable at the time…nobody likes it in the beginning because of the separation," he adds, searching for the words to explain what it's like to go from one existence to another without any control over any of it, and then finding yourself in the unique position of having to start over to rebuild a new definition of happiness.

"A lot of the free time we had, we'd climb trees and catch squirrels.

We carried them around in our pockets, made them pets, particularly flying squirrels. We'd sail them back and forth between each other.

"Or take a bed sheet and some pine about six or seven feet long and a tub and go sailing, and we'd go anywhere we wanted to in those days. We'd get in the Baby Hole (a small inlet alongside Moon River) and turn a boat over and get up under in the air pocket and smoke until Mr. Corry would knock on the boat and say, 'you come out of there.'"

Claude Corry took care of the cows and taught the boys how to do the same. They rose at 5:30 a.m. and plowed the fields or milked the cows. Glaen was on cow duty for a long time. "We knew we weren't going to sit on our duffs and somebody would take care of us. I did know I was loved. Mr. Corry, if you had a problem, he'd come talk to you. He'd take care of things. He was like a dad to me and I told him so."

Over time, Glaen came to love the place and the land. "People would pay a thousand a week to go stay out there in the countryside with an Olympic-size pool and horses. We had all that," he said.

He briefly took part in World War II, after leaving Bethesda, joining the Navy, and serving in Okinawa. He was headed for Japan and China for the great invasion when someone on his ship noticed they were traveling in circles. The entire seventh fleet. A new invention, the atom bomb, had been dropped on Japan, and he was returning home.

Retired from Sears back in Savannah, he serves on the board of governors for Bethesda now and makes a point of talking to the current residents, fellow Bethesda Boys, to help ease the transition into a new way of life. "I tell them how wonderful this place is and they believe it after I get through talking to them. Just about every one of them I've seen out there has progressed in their life and have a good attitude and know that they're learning."

Years after he was at Bethesda, his mother apologized for sending him, saying she was sorry. "I said, you did the best you could, and told her not to feel badly. One Sunday a month she'd come out and visit. And the beauty of the land. It was like a dream out there."

Once a month, just like other families who gather together around long tables for Sunday suppers, Glaen has all the alumni in town over to his house in a celebration of his extended family.

"Our greatest glory is not in never falling, but in rising every time we fall."

Confucius

There is a class-action suit making its way state-by-state across the country that is challenging the legality of placing any child whose legal guardian is the state, a foster child, into a residential care facility. So far the law in Tennessee has been changed to exclude residential education facilities, and Georgia shortly followed suit after my visit to make the suit go away. However, despite repeated invitations, none of the critics from the state legislature has ever set foot on the Bethesda Home for Boys campus in Savannah to see what might be lost or gained and by whom. One large loss was their decision in March of 2007 to stop taking boys from social services. The profile of the boys I met was before the decision. Many of the politicians who lessened the options don't know the difference between residential education and residential treatment.

The suit's central argument is that all children deserve a home of their own, and short of that, whatever most closely resembles that. Anything less than that will provoke a lawsuit. It sounds great, but look behind the platitudes at the reality thousands of children are left to deal with while a lot of adults keep their focus on what they can't achieve. But look only if you're ready for a very lonely and very hot seat.

We could always point out the obvious holes in the lawsuit's argument: there aren't enough adoptive homes or foster families to place most of the children, and a lot of the children, due to continual reassignment and the nightmare they were removed from in the first place, need more wrap-around care than foster care can provide. But if you raise these objections be prepared to be labeled as one who is against the American family of two parents, one house, and a few happy, well-adjusted kids. Mention the pragmatic facts of the story, that for years residential facilities have been operating on less public money yet were forced to provide more services, and expect worse names to follow.

So far in this debate, no one's been allowed to point out the reality.

The argument of last resort by people who want to win without being closely scrutinized is, "if you're not for us, you're against us." It's very effective, particularly if it can be mixed with religion, patriotism, or a vulnerable population.

The staff at Bethesda Home for Boys, a home with a little over 100 boys, forty in residential care and sixty-five boys as day students, with an average length of stay of eighteen months for the boys in residence, knows a little bit about being on the wrong side of that argument. David Tribble, the executive director of the Bethesda Home and an ordained Baptist minister, came to the home in 1991 from the Ellen Hines Smith Girls Home in Spartanburg, South Carolina, where he was the executive director. "I visited Bethesda and saw a really attractive opportunity," he said. Shortly, he will step down from the day to day operations as director and take on fundraising for the home full-time.

The campus sits on 650 acres of rural landscape alongside the Moon River dotted with ancient live oak trees dripping with Spanish

The entrance to the Bethesda Home for Boys.

moss. Near the river's edge is an old plaque commemorating the first baptism in 1763. Rev. Nicholas Bedgegood baptized Benjamin Stirk and his wife Mary, Mr. Dupree, Mrs. Hannah Barksdale Polhill, and numerous others.

In the recent past, the home served as a dairy farm, and the boys all had chores that included taking care of the cows. The home still has heads of cattle that the boys help out with, but several activities, such as riding horses, have been curtailed due to rising insurance costs. The age range at Bethesda was wider then with boys starting as young as six years old, but no one over 14 was admitted and all were privately placed. But, in 1991, with the advent of young men from social services who came in with more emotional issues, it was thought to not be in the best interests of the younger boys to remain at Bethesda.

The boys who live here now range in age from twelve to eighteen in four cottages that have no more than ten boys in each one and are manned by a mix of men and women who rotate shifts. There used to be a system of house parents, much like the Virginia home, but now, no house parent lives full-time in the cottages anymore, and one of the cottages is currently closed because of a lack of resources. The three that are open date from 1938, 1940, and 1976, respectively, and are a little in need of updating.

Boys who lived here in the 1940s and '50s, like Glaen Richards, were known to create sailboats out of a tub, a stick, and a sheet and take off down the river for Ossabaw Sound about eight miles away where the water becomes salty. They'd pull the little makeshift boat into a marsh and lie down in the mud, contemplating the world. Or turn the boat over in the small inlet fondly known as the Baby Hole and duck up underneath to get into mischief and smoke. Any adult passing by though knew what was going on and were prone to bang on the top till heads reemerged. The oldest living alum is Robert Fears at ninety-three years old, and he lives nearby.

Half Rubber Ball, a game the alumni swear they invented and still bring back every Anniversary Day when thousands appear for the events and picnics, was played with half a rubber ball and a broom handle. The pitcher threw it sidearm, making it hard to hit. They still love it.

Climbing in the tall live oak trees so they could catch baby flying squirrels by placing a shirt over the nest and carrying the entire thing down was also a favorite past time. The squirrels were nursed and made into pets that they carried around in their pockets or sent sailing between boys as they walked along. It was a different era before insurance or thoughts about what young men ought to be doing.

Beginning in 1991, the home started taking in boys from foster care, which meant their legal guardian was the state, and because of that, lately they've been taking it on the chin.

There are 16,000 kids in foster care in Georgia, many of whom are in a constant state of transition. A good number of them are from rural areas in the state where there are still a lot of wide open spaces. That means many localities outside of big cities like Atlanta had fewer homes to draw from in the first place that might want to take in foster children. The options for these children were sparse.

The Bethesda Home, a fixture of Savannah before the town had a name, saw the local need (75 percent of the children in their care are from the surrounding community) and changed their long-standing policy of private placements only. They were following the trend of the early 1990s when it became obvious that the foster care system was overburdened and breaking down. The number of children needing a safe place to be increased sharply as the number of families willing to take them in kept declining. Children were warehoused in shelters and corners were cut on background checks of possible families. Horror stories about foster care abuses started to appear on local and national news. There were stories of children being bounced a dozen times from home to home, encountering abuse and neglect. Foster care had become the new Dickensian reality for children without roots.

In response to the national crisis and the documented success of established residential education facilities, new residential education facilities were opened in the largest wave since the turn of the twentieth century. Old homes like Bethesda rethought their policies and made room for the children who were failing out of foster care.

Now, these homes like Bethesda are squarely in the center of the argument and are being painted as the villain. Not because of poor results or visits to Bethesda's leafy campus, but because it couldn't offer each child a separate home of his own. Of course, the foster care system couldn't provide enough homes either, but not enough people pointed that out.

"They're sending a lot of kids back to places before anybody's ready," said David Tribble. "We see kids where pressure is applied.

[The kids are told they] should want to move back into foster care or back in with their family. The case manager can then close the books on them and lower the rolls. It improves their success rate," he said.

He points out the recent case of a teenage boy who was sexually abused by his mother's boyfriend, who was subsequently convicted and sent to jail. For a while, the boy was sent to Bethesda, where he received treatment and started to put his life back together. But, now the sexual offender is out of prison and back in the house and the state wants to return the boy to the family. The mother wants to keep the boyfriend.

David has argued with the case manager on behalf of the boy, but to no avail. "The case workers are saying this guy has done what the state requires of him and are 'keeping a close eye on him,'" says David. The child is the one who will be taking the chances, and the file will be closed. The child was returned to his home.

Often, someone's real intentions can be seen in what's not said or done. No one who wants the bill passed in Georgia, and then duplicated in other states, is arguing against sending children who cross the line of violence to a juvenile detention hall. It's a more important distinction than is first evident. Without the wrap-around care these residential facilities provide, a lot of the children who have been pushed out of foster care might find themselves in the only available housing left—a detention center.

What will be difficult to watch are the tragedies that will result if the proposals are enacted. Residential education facilities will no longer be an option, despite the homes proven success at raising happy, independent adults.

The word "Bethesda" means "Home of Mercy" and comes from the Bible. It's as good a place as any to start the story of this home that has survived both man-made and natural disasters over the past centuries. They've been burned, blown down by hurricane, divided during the American Revolution and then the Civil War, and have fought back other attempts to break them up by legislature now long-gone—and they are still standing. Bethesda continues its mission of taking in boys from around Georgia who are in need of a place to call home.

"Bethesda was in existence 160 years before the first child welfare law was passed. We've stood the test of time. We've been taking care of children before there was a city to ask us to," he said, as a little of the weariness and frustration began showing around the edges. Guiding teenage boys to adulthood is tough enough, but add in the behavioral and emotional issues they come with, and then the political battles on top of it all, and his weariness is easy to understand.

"One of the main things we have to overcome is that we look traditional," he said, referring to the large green expanse dotted with older stately buildings that surround a large center of grass; all of it offset by the tall trees. "'It's an orphanage. It's warehousing kids.' How do you know it's a warehouse? Why do you have programs with seven or eight kids in foster homes? Why is that not a warehouse?" he asks. "We have roughly seventy-five or eighty men [former residents] who come to celebrate every year and can wax eloquently about the place." David is pointing this out because none of the political critics have ever set foot on the grounds of Bethesda, but they have plenty to say, and no one is asking the alumni for their opinion. It's all become weirdly lopsided.

We set out for lunch in town, taking along three young men, all residents of the home, who David has wanted to have the chance to check in with, to hear how they're doing. I'm along for the ride.

James is in tenth grade at Bethesda and has been at the home for four years. He's a left guard on the football team with ambitions of studying communications or real estate. Damon is in eleventh grade, has also been at Bethesda for four years, and is interested in mass communication or becoming an actor or comedian. He is the most talkative of the trio with a quick wit. He looks like he's always on the verge of breaking into a smile. Not too long ago he earned $350 from the sale of an abstract painting he created and used the money to rent a tiger outfit for the first football game. It was the best pick of the costumes. He was determined that the school would have a mascot, and he spent the game charging up and down the sidelines. His enthusiasm is infectious and now there is talk about coming up with a real mascot for the Blazers, the name of the team. Maybe a dragon.

Daniel, who is also in the eleventh grade and has been at the home the longest, since he was six years old, fixes me with the most direct look. He came to the home with a brother two years older who has recently graduated. He misses him, he says. He is deep waters, thoughtful and distant, and tells me he doesn't plan to ever get married. It's difficult to tell if he's tired of my questions or really means it.

David has brought these boys together to ask them what they think about getting rid of the level system. It's a behavior modification program similar to what is used at Happy Hill Farm, in which the residents earn points through a combination of age, behavior, and grades that allows them to move to a higher level that equates with more privileges. It's also possible, through grades or behavior, to move down a level. David's considering going to a Restorative Model used by a home in Connecticut, where the home will go to for training once the new director is in place. The Model uses individual attention by staff members when a child is upset to try and understand first the child's point of view and second to help the child see other potential outcomes. An emphasis is also placed on helping the child to take more personal responsibility and make amends when necessary. The hope is that this model would emphasize building relationships, a skill most boys who arrive on campus lack but will need to master in order to become successful in general. Other goals in the new system are how to make relationships work for you, and if something negative happens how to restore the relationship. David thinks it's a better model to teach the boys how to get along in the world once they have graduated.

He asks the boys what they think and they warm to the subject, giving thoughtful answers about what they already like and would hate to lose. The boys like the privileges they've earned through the level system but say the rules aren't always evenly meted out. Maybe a new system would allow for more even-handed assessments. They weigh the pros and cons and have forgotten I'm sitting there, focused on David and the topic at hand. David is genuinely interested in what they say, taking their opinions to heart.

Another welcome change is the $140,000 renovation of the old laundry facility into a state of the art studio with two bays for filming and a control room. John Jackson, who used to work for an NBC affiliate, runs the show. Boys can learn about broadcasting by helping with filming local school and town council meetings and airing them over Channel 17 through the Bethesda Comcast Alliance, part of the Comcast company. They also air local religious programming from area churches, which brings in some revenue and provides additional experience.

There are still adventures that have the simplicity of the past, however, as there are in any rural setting. Mickey Minick, director of student support services, a tall man who is legendary on campus, and Jeff Walker, director of Youth Enterprise Systems (YES), could tell about a few of them. Jeff, forty-three years old and married for eight years to Linda, runs something on campus called Character Camp which is the first phase of the YES program. During camp, boys get male mentors and get to work off-campus to learn about how to show up on time and be prepared with the right attitude. "I think it's going to help with anger levels," said Mickey.

One year, Mickey, who's always up for a challenge, baited the younger Jeff into trying to swim across the river. Men being boys in taller packages, he accepted, and while the boys all watched from the sidelines wearing life jackets and lifeguards kept their eyes on everyone, the two men took off for the swim.

Mickey, who is fifty years old, cruised through the water without even breathing hard while Jeff began finding a closer relationship to God and asking for help, while listening for every little sound or move-

Enjoying the Moon River.

ment. It's a river that's known to have snakes or alligators. There are even stories of an occasional lost shark. Both of them made it back just fine. Mickey says he'd do it again. Jeff is pretty sure he won't.

However, the next night the two of them did take out a canoe looking for alligators whose eyes glow green in the beam of a flashlight. Jeff had to know. "We didn't see any, but if we had we would have gone back in the water the next day, anyway."

It's a rural area. If they worried about wildlife no one would go out. It does cut down on anyone trying to suddenly leave at night, though, with fox, deer, and raccoons wandering the campus.

Alligators, or gators as they're called, have been known to venture up on to the campus, and when they do a local company, Critter Gitter, is called to come and capture the uninvited guest and put him back in the wildlife a little farther away.

Down a long dirt road about a mile from the main campus is the barn with the cows. Gators have been known to wander back there looking for dinner, but the last one who tried it was found in a staring contest with a cow in which neither one blinked. Critter Gitter was called.

The day after the swimming contest the boys were back in the water with Mickey and Jeff creeping underneath to grab at ankles. Boy fun. And also one of the better ways they bond.

My WASP-ish father and Louie used to have burping contests in the kitchen almost every morning. Dad always won, he could do the alphabet. And they had endless jokes they never let me hear but delighted in mumbling if I passed through the room. When Louie was only three, Dad would wear a Ninja Turtle mask and sneak up behind him to suddenly surprise him. Louie would collapse in terror before shrieking with delight, asking Granddaddy to do it again. Males have a different language that is more physical than verbal and is formed as much in play as it is in working side by side. Both are important.

Sometimes, boys have a way of finding both. Walking back across the campus one afternoon, I stop to watch a small group of middle schoolers who are "helping out" by trimming a large and very wide row of tall bushes under the careful supervision of assistant football coach Clevan Thompson, an imposing figure. Most of the hedges are taller than the boys, but it's still possible to see where they've been by the holes and topography that now bears a resemblance to a mountain range. The exercise is more about pitching in and helping out. Professional ground crews generally tend to the grounds. Most of the boys are very serious about their mission, even though are still occasionally running back to their teacher to see if they can bargain for extra time in the gym in return for their diligence before returning to the hedge.

"We'll see, we'll see," he answers patiently, every time. Eventually they are rounded up and head off happily to chase basketballs. Work and play.

Bill McIlrath Sr., or Mr. Mac, as the kids call him, hails from western Pennsylvania but speaks in a soft southern drawl and is the other side of the equation, providing the balance as an older male role model who works to get the boys to be consistent and have a good work ethic. He has been at Bethesda for 35 years, brought here by his brother in law, Bill Ford, a former Bethesda boy who married Mr. Mac's sister.

Mr. Mac bonds with the boys while working side-by-side with them, mostly in the 24,000 square-foot Agri-Science Center built in 2004 for $3.2 million, all local money. Right now, there are twenty-two cows in the barn—twenty of them are heifers, and all are pregnant. He tried valiantly at one point to get the boys interested in taking care of their own cow, buying calves for each interested boy, but it didn't take and he ended up with the job himself. However, it didn't stop him from trying.

He decided to try something easier, something smaller, like chickens. Irish McCormick, the thirty-six-year-old principal of the school, remembers the chickens.

She started on the campus as a substitute and had only been there three weeks when the boys convinced her they needed to clean out the coops before class. A standard ploy for substitutes but with an outdoor twist. "The kids opened up the coop and chickens went everywhere," she said, smiling, a little wiser now. "I thought, 'oh, these people are going to fire me.'" It turns out the boys had done it before.

The cows, which are used as food on the campus as well as to generate funds to keep Bethesda going, still need tending. A small knot of boys has come down the road with Mr. Mac to help him out and learn a little bit. They are dutifully sweeping out the ramps and cement floors around the barn, waiting for inspection by Mr. Mac, who is busy using a forklift to feed the cows.

He has to corral both cows and boys a few times to get back to their respective tasks but eventually every one is happy and he gives them the promised ride in the shovel of the forklift, raising them a few feet off the ground and driving a short way down the road, setting them on a small pile of hay. They sit enthralled, marveling at the view. Afterward, everybody gets in Mr. Mac's truck to go and fetch sodas as he talks to them about what a good job they've done and how much he appreciates their help and hard work. This is good parenting. The kind that slides in when no one is really looking and is an art that Mr. Mac has down. He gives the boys validation for who they are—not because of what they're doing, that's a side lesson of respect—but because they just are, and he doesn't withhold it either until a child is doing what he wants them to do. They always possess his respect even if he's fussing at them to get back to work and stop the fooling around. Responsibility and self-worth are separate issues. The first a child takes on, building the list as they mature. The second is innately theirs to keep and discover, building on as well.

This being the South, with a capital S, the other way males bond and learn is through football. Coach Antwain Turner, who is muscled and compact with a perpetual smile, has been slowly teaching the boys how to play since he arrived at Bethesda in 2002 as a residential cottage worker before becoming a teacher. Three years ago he started flag football, and everybody came out and had a great time. At the time the only team sport on campus was basketball. If you didn't play basketball you didn't have an opportunity to play organized sports.

When football was recently introduced, many of the kids had never played before. "We were their first team. They didn't know the rules, didn't watch it on TV," he said. Now, a lot of the boys sit down together to watch a whole game and are overheard saying, "I want to be the best."

"Big time change," said Coach Turner, as he talked about the same wall that I've heard Mickey mention. The wall the boys had faced many times before and walked away from. Getting them over that is key to unlocking their potential. "It's not where you start, its how you finish. These kids are not only accustomed to quitting, they're accustomed to people quitting on them. We've had a lot of opportunities to throw in the towel and when we didn't, it surprised them," he said.

"Sports are a big motivator because if you want to play football it's a requirement to get an education. Probably about two or three years ago college was far-fetched. A lot of the guys would pick up trades. A lot now see maybe they do have a chance at college." It was a daisy chain effect. They wanted to be on the field so they tried a little harder in class. The success in class led to a hope of going further, beyond Bethesda.

It has helped that they've had their first success story, Ben Green, who earned a scholarship to Edward Waters College in Jacksonville, Florida. His acceptance into college has made it more believable for everyone who comes after him. "He had a lot of things against him and Ben was driven because he saw the door crack open for him. The staff laid out a path for him. If he was motivated then he could achieve at an optimum level," said Coach.

When the opportunity to start the football program arose in 2004, Coach Turner was overwhelmed with joy to be in that position. It's what makes him perfect for the job. He didn't look at what might be an overwhelming task—starting a program from a limited pool of boys who've never even watched an entire game, much less played one. He didn't see a wall and back away—he built a ladder and took the boys with him.

"At twenty-seven to be a head football coach with a starter program and build a foundation for years to come; to be a teacher on the field and help the kids learn from their mistakes and their triumphs…" He stops talking, choking up over his gratitude to be able to contribute something that will last long after he's gone.

But he has to work overtime to keep them motivated. In 2006, early in the season a tenth grader was removed from the team, but not without working through some issues first and walking away having learned something.

The tenth grader missed an excessive number of practices. He apologized and made up the work, but after they lost the game he did it again and acted out in his cottage, which led to his temporary suspension from the team. He hit that wall, and he and Coach Turner had a conversation about working on priorities right now.

Coach Turner keeps looking for ways to motivate everyone he can. Daniel had been one of those young men who needed some motivation. He was used to being listened to, not doing so much of the listening. During the team's first season, he made a point of talking it down and trying to see who he could get to go along with him. He's a natural leader and got some of the younger players to start thinking about quitting. This is the worst kind of wave that can come over any new idea and swamp it.

Daniel was told he couldn't be a part of the team if he didn't change his attitude. There's an old saying that when one door closes, another one opens … but being in the hallway is the hard part. That was Daniel's hallway. He decided to apologize and come back to practice, doing the extra workouts to show the other players he was willing to operate as one of the team and pull together.

"Two of our juniors have an opportunity to go to University of Georgia's football camp and talk to the head coach, Mark Rick," bringing their enthusiasm back to their team mates. "It made my job a little easier this year. We made the transition from eight-man to eleven-man football this year and more kids see we are building a system here and they have an opportunity to go somewhere," said Coach Turner.

"My dream is that, number one, every kid will really know and understand they have a purpose in life and, number two, their duty and obligation is to fulfill that. Some day we'll have a stadium here, an increased enrollment, get at least fifty players to a team ..."

He is starting with what he has, building the foundation, and preparing for what he dreams of—eventually more boys benefiting from football and going on to college.

The school day is over, and Coach Turner has to head over to the field behind the baseball field for football practice. He expects thirteen out of the twenty young men who should be there to show up, even though the first game of the season is tomorrow against Westwood, and it counts. But nineteen out of twenty are already there ahead of Coach Turner, throwing the ball to each other. Tomorrow matters to them. Playing college football matters more and keeps them from quitting. Daniel, the young man from lunch, has said, "That's the dream."

Before the coach had arrived, another player, trying to pump everybody up for what's to come tomorrow, had been trying out a little trash-talking and was shouting very close to Daniel's face, through his helmet. It's enough to cause a fight just about anywhere, but Daniel is telling the other player, in very measured words, to back off.

"You need to stop," he says, over and over, loud enough for me to hear on the sidelines sitting on the old wooden bleachers. But he never shoves, never even raises an arm in any kind of gesture. He has become a mature leader.

Coach comes in on the end of it and tells the other player to go take a break off the field. The young man tries to explain his misguided attempts at team spirit, but there are consequences. Time to go take a break. He walks off steamed, but he'll be back. The team matters.

Coach calls out to the team. "Bring it in, bring it in." They circle near him, shoulder to shoulder in their new uniforms as a prayer is given before practice. Their hands are on each others' shoulders, connecting all of them, as each holds his blue helmet in the other hand.

A collective "amen" rises up as fists touch in the air all around.

"One—two—three," calls out Coach Turner, and the boys give a low grunt. They're off to practice being a team and coming together for a common mission—get over another wall together.

So many of the boys come from single-parent homes headed by a woman, just like Louie, that there is a real need for the building of these close, positive male role models, which can put an extra burden on the coaches, male teachers, and especially the house dads who make up half of the teaching parents who live in the homes with the boys.

"It definitely was a level of responsibility," said Mickey, who used to be a house parent at Bethesda with his wife of 22 years, Jenny. "Even when you're tired and don't want to go talk to a child, you knew how important it was. It may be about sports, about something they saw in the news. It meant the world to them." So you go.

It reminds me of all the parent teacher nights I've attended with bleary-eyed parents crammed into little desks listening to what their child was going to learn in United States history this year. We were all exhausted, but we knew it was important to be involved, and if we got home and our child wanted to talk to us for a few minutes before they fell asleep, we'd sit down next to them and listen. There were more than a few nights that I fell asleep next to Louie after reading him a story and then listening to him tell me about his day. I'd wake up, my neck sore from falling asleep propped up, and still feel the same awe I had when he was first born.

The issues the boys confront now—abuse, drugs, and alcohol for example—make the opportunities to chat even more important. They have had some trust broken, and they're going to check out everyone who comes into their life based on criteria that's important to them, said Mickey. "Making a bond here is critical."

It can help them to learn to push beyond the limited successes they've experienced in the past to risk failure or defeat and find out how to achieve. "When the going gets tough, they don't keep going," says Mickey. "It's a fear of failure. It's frustrating that they'll walk away from it. Not all of them. For the older ones, it's hard. Not going to happen overnight. They have a strong habit, but if we can keep them for at least two years, maybe three ... plant a seed. We're not going to be able to tell though for five years. Then you just have to trust in the Lord."

Most of the boys walk in thinking they're here for the short term and then they'll be headed back home. But, like the other residential education facilities, some stay just long enough to gain a reference point of how things could be and if they do leave early, sometimes, they end up calling to see if their bed is still available.

Jay, days away from turning seventeen, is an articulate young man, tall and slight, with thin wire glasses and bright white sneakers. He now attends a private prep school off the grounds of Bethesda, paid for by the home. He came to Bethesda determined to find a different way of dealing with life. He was living in a household with an adult who suffered from chronic and serious mood swings. He wanted something better for himself and he was determined to get it.

"When you're little, and that's the force that's raising you, it's hard when your grandmother is bipolar. My grandmother would be really happy one moment and dejected the next," he said.

"I'd ride my bike along a two-lane highway to night school with cars whizzing by and my grandmother's at home wishing me dead because I didn't clean the kitchen fast enough. That plays on your mind," he said, stressing every word.

"Now, I have my license. I got it while I've been here. I have a pool table in my room," he said checking off the benefits. But what he sees as the biggest benefit is how consistent everyone is with their behavior. He likens it to stepping out of a circle of negativity that had been passed down in his family for generations. He sees himself as the break in the chain, as a new tree.

The walls of the cottages where the boys live tell a story about how successful the home has been at working with boys from foster care. There are dents and dings and small holes patched over here and there. More signs of wear than I've seen at other places like Girard or Happy Hill that don't take in children from social services.

The boys arrive at Bethesda with their anger intact and learn quickly that they can no longer take it out on each other. A new system of learning how to express anger or frustration constructively is preached and eventually absorbed.

At any of these homes, the new patterns are a system of substitutions replacing old, negative behavior or beliefs with new choices. But, the boys have had ten or twelve years of practicing the old ways and it takes time to trust, bond, and start to practice something new consistently. "The big challenge in our cottages is to get kids to take care of the property. The boys don't have a concept this is where they live, this is where they're staying. They have been moved around a lot and these kids are modeling adult behavior they've seen," said David Tribble.

In the meantime, taking any aggression out on each other is not tolerated in any way, and almost every boy who comes here has a desire to change, so they're trying something new, but the anger has to go somewhere.

The walls take the brunt of it. "Cottages get more beat up now," said Mickey. "we don't have a lot of fighting. They'll trash talk but they're good kids. They'll take it out on a trash can, or a wall."

The holes in the wall are a dot-to-dot pattern of optimism dug into the wall. It's a first step toward letting go and allowing something else to take place.

That's another key lesson I've learned during my travels this year. Don't judge anything on face value because there is a hidden treasure everywhere. But if I'm so locked into what I believe or hold fast to my illusion of standards, I'll miss it.

It's what David Tribble believes has happened in the political halls of Georgia. Too many politicians have bought into what they have heard, but not seen.

David couldn't see all of that when he first came to visit the home. All he knew was the sterling reputation that was writ large, and he took it a little for granted that everyone else in the state knew, too.

"I was thirty-seven years old and I recognized the challenges, but I was pretty naïve about what those challenges were."

Bethesda Home received a large endowment in 1972 that allowed the board the leeway to make the decision to stop fundraising and support the home entirely with income from the endowment. Every person who runs a non-profit organization has the daydream of securing an endowment large enough so that there are no more wine and cheese soirees or mass mailers or crunching numbers to come up with annual budgets and hoping there's enough money to support every item.

But there's another reason fundraising is such an important element of any campus, especially a home. It requires not only staying open to the public, but actively inviting the community in to take a look around, get to know everybody, and become friends and allies. That way, when trouble rolls into town, everyone already knows each other and is comfortable and feels invested.

In 1991, when David arrived on the grounds of Bethesda, passing under the stately large arch at the end of a long road, he didn't realize there weren't enough people making the trip, and many people had started to pass right by the home, not realizing it was even there anymore. That's not a good thing.

"They had been kind of hidden for thirty years," said David. "We had to get back out in the front of the community again and start a fund drive." Even with its long fabled history of child care, it wasn't easy. And to complicate matters, Bethesda was slowly losing its public charity status. Every public charity is required by the I.R.S. to raise a certain percentage of their funds from the public domain. Bethesda wasn't meeting that quota.

But, as I'd heard from so many people during this year of change, what can seem like the darkest moment can turn out to be the best day, because it was when you were *finally* ready to listen. That's what happened to Bethesda.

In 1991, the school not only started taking in boys from foster care, but it also integrated, allowing in boys of color, and moved the residential education facility in to the present culture. The home arrived a little later to civil rights than others, but it got there.

However, the political timing of adding in children from social services quickly turned into an argument with the state, and whether or not this turns out to be a *best day* is still to be seen. "When political action groups came to Georgia either we as providers were truly asleep at the switch … We knew they were suing the state, but we thought it was over shelters. And how an attorney general and Department of Human Resources can make sweeping changes based on two overcrowded emergency children's shelters and didn't consult anyone in residential education facilities …" said David, still looking dazed from all of the pronouncements. The lawsuits filed by independent child advocate groups were the first instance of the controversy reaching the attention of the homes. The public still seemed unaware.

The state requires that no child under twelve can be in congregant care, and no child can be place more than fifty miles from their home. All of this sounds like a good idea, but it turned out to be the old story of every child deserves a family of his own while turning a blind eye to the paucity of actual families, whether they are foster care or adoptive. "We're dealing with the pretend families Georgia keeps jettisoning up; that the state talks about as a better alternative. It's the pretend factor and the kids know that," said David. In other words, the state is talking about an ideal that doesn't exist, offering up foster families they don't have.

And, with so much of Georgia still rural, it can make it tough in some counties to find a good foster care family within fifty miles of a child's home. However, it ensures that many children won't have a chance to benefit from Bethesda Home.

"There was a bunker mentality in the capital," said David. The outside groups started throwing litigation at Georgia, and officials started giving in to make the suits go away. "We've seen a tremendous amount of loss with referrals from DHR [Department of Human Resources]." Social workers are telling Bethesda the children they're suddenly seeing have too many problems, their behavioral problems are too severe. However, they will fit into a private foster care home where there is less training. "All I know is there's a sudden loss in volume," he said. When he looked to the future, David saw the possibility arising where they will stop taking children from social services and go back to just private placements.

"I don't have a dog in this fight. We've only been taking in kids from foster care since 1991. You don't get to tell a non-profit who they are. What they don't realize is we have a board to report to, a community, a mission.

"For us, the big issue is continuity of care longer than thirty, sixty, or ninety days. We follow our kids for two years or more to make sure they're okay. The other way [foster care], there's no way to know the impact. Kids are revolving through and are only temporarily stabilized."

Lately, there's even been an internal struggle about the exact name of the home. Some of the on-site school, The Bethesda School's, parents and board members think the name should be The Bethesda Home & School for Boys.

"But everyone needs to feel like they're from someplace," said David. "If you lose the word 'home' you lose a big part of the culture here."

What is lost is the focus on the children who need them the most, the ones without a home, and the core mission to raise the bar for all the children who live on campus. Rather than focus solely on the type

Working in the computer lab.

of home, like the state has legislated, focus on what the children have been gaining from what exists and keep what's already working for the children in the state of Georgia. Just like any of the other homes I visited, it is vital to emphasize consistently that more is expected of the resident children than they're used to, because the adults at the home know that each child can do it. Raise the expectation, raise the self-esteem, and down the line, you raise the quality of life these kids build for themselves out there on their own.

Each child comes to believe he deserves more and is capable of achieving it. David is refusing to give up on his mission. He reminds me of some of the people I knew when I was growing up at the seminary in Virginia. Those people who were willing to risk everything to change what they believed needed to be changed, even if it meant social isolation or veiled threats. And most of them were never written about or ballyhooed, but their contributions helped add up to a law being passed or to the next generation having it a bit easier.

Every child who comes to Bethesda and gets the chance to stay long enough to figure things out and recover from the fractured family they left behind owes something to David and his staff. Every child who then goes on to college and a new kind of a life than their family tree may ever have known before has people like David to thank. Or like Mr. Mac.

"There's an awful lot of people here with strong academic backgrounds who are very capable of doing many other things and being compensated far more handsomely," said David. They're here by choice and have high expectations of the kids and themselves.

Like the school principal Irish McCormick, whose voice can be heard over the school intercom throughout the day making announcements. The children love and respect her; the younger ones stop by the office to show her a test score or pull her out into the hall to see how they've decorated a bulletin board.

A boy sails by wearing Spock ears as Mickey, in "Mr. Minick" mode

The academic building.

as director of student support services, tells him to remove them and move on to class. The children swirl by, trying to get somewhere on time.

Upstairs in the main building in Miss Vera Fish's class, the first through fourth grade are mixed together in a small group. They sit together according to their grade but at any given moment someone is up and moving around, mostly Jason who is in fourth grade and loves to help out. "Not right now," says Miss Fish, and not for the first time, as she sends Jason back to his seat.

Earlier at lunch there was a hitting incident between the younger boys that took place so quickly witnesses were scarce. Feelings took the brunt of it and there is a careful reenactment to try and parse out the real offender. Eventually, everyone has to shake hands and apologize and we make a small little train of people heading back to the school building. Miss Fish is very good at keeping all of the fellows together without ever bellowing. And they don't make it easy. A butterfly darts near us and is enough to send a few running after it, completely lost in the chase. She gently calls them back, and we set off again.

It's the same way back in the classroom. It is a marvel to watch how often the boys get up and pop back down during an exercise, and yet, somehow, after it's all over, every one has completed their work. I was sitting there with them, and I still wasn't sure how that happened.

She gives me a patient smile and goes back to talking to the boys.

Back in Ms. McCormack's office, she is busy making small goodie bags for the football team before they head off for the first official game as an eleven-man team against a very tough rival. The Blazers are pumped up and heading off to the bus as she says a quick goodbye and offers a few words of football-style encouragement.

She describes herself as a former military brat from Columbia, South Carolina, who had ambitions of becoming an attorney, not a teacher. But, life has a way of helping out with choices.

After her son Sydney, now thirteen, came along she found herself managing a children's fine apparel shop and saw the blessings in having work hours that matched her school-age child. So she went for her teacher's certification.

Some of the children have managed to get closer to her than others, especially Daniel, the football team leader. She has known him since he arrived at Bethesda and has pictures of the small boy riding a horse, a large smile on his face, or at an annual Christmas pageant. Three years ago when his mother died, she accompanied him and his older brother to the funeral, shepherding them through the ordeal.

"He's just now learning how to have high expectations for himself. He's just now starting to become a leader," she said, noticing the same qualities as Coach Turner. "Sports has drawn that character out of him. He used to be that student that would hide, almost invisible. Every now and then he would speak to let you know he was still around."

I spot him the next day cutting up with some other students, sharing a joke, but then he sees me and straightens up, nodding his head in my direction, dropping the smile. We don't share that trust, and there isn't enough time for us to build any. Not the time Daniel would need, but it's okay. He has people like Irish, who said she doesn't know how long she'll be at Bethesda but she knows she'll be there at least long enough to watch Daniel graduate.

Deborah Gibbons, forty-seven years old—my age—has a different perspective than most of the other adults who work at Bethesda. She was raised in foster care and abused by her biological family and had to overcome all of the same issues to arrive where she's at today. "That's what gives me the strength to work with these kids. They have a reason for acting out and it's not you. It's up to us to come up with a plan, don't get drawn into content." Not get distracted by the anger the kids arrive with.

She is now the weekday residential supervisor and has been at Bethesda for almost seven years. She's studying to become an ordained minister and is in outreach ministry. She sees the calling as part of the necessary package for anyone who wants to work at a residential education facility.

"It's a great job because God has me here," she said, surrendering the need to analyze things from every angle. "What impresses me about this place is the history behind it. The staff and the boys were all white," until David Tribble's arrival in 1991. "That in itself is special to me. I read in the archives about George Whitfield," the founder. "He established a negro college. . . . Opposition came from the clergy back in the 1700s," she said, drawing a thread of history from the beginning of the country to her part in it now.

"When I first got here, if I had gotten caught up in 'no blacks in administration,' what would have changed? Instead, I spoke up about not being modeled, and they came back and offered me the position.

"You're not only talking the problem here, you're talking the solution and I'm being part of the solution," she said.

Being part of the solution is a trickier component than it appears at face value, at least back in my own home. I had stopped going out of town for a while, after traveling to Texas to visit the Happy Hill Farm Academy. I had to let go and be okay with coming to a stop. That was new. I was used to being driven by outside deadlines, outside expectations from editors or family members.

It was late May, 2006, when I got back from Texas and was confronted with the truth. Louie's drinking was not only out of hand. It was more than a problem. It was alcoholism. He had inherited the disease from his father and it was now full-blown.

I was finally at a place where I'd been pushed to an understanding that if I were to keep going right at that moment I was going to have to allow Louie to hit bottom on his own and all the loss that might entail. I wasn't there yet.

There were remnants of a sober Louie left and I used them for as long as I could to get him through the last days of high school and on to graduation.

I confronted him about the beer and took away his cell phone and the keys to his car. He handed them over, but not before punching his fist through his closet door, ranting and raving upstairs, and threatening to walk out and not come back. I stood on the stairs and quietly kept saying he couldn't leave, amazed that he wasn't just pushing past me. I knew if he left we'd have crossed another line and we weren't there yet.

Losing the phone mattered to him and he asked how he could get it back sooner than the two weeks I had prescribed. It was a measure of my insanity that I set any kind of time limit, as though being grounded was going to *cure* any of this.

"Go to an AA meeting," I said. It wasn't a thought I'd had a moment before I said it, but he leapt at it so I looked up meeting times. We agreed on a Tuesday night, a few days away. I started driving him to school to make sure he got there, and I plotted with his principal behind his back to ground him in-school as well. He was stuck in a room for days with nothing but the late work to complete, which put him back on schedule for graduation. Louie had said he was already having blackouts from the alcohol and I knew he wasn't going to trust his memory enough to believe he hadn't done something to earn an in-school suspension for the three days it took to get him caught up.

In a quiet room with only a proctor and nothing to do all day—even lunch was in that small room—he steadily worked at the pile of material till it was all completed. It even had the added benefit of helping him to study for exams. It turned out to be some of his best work and showed what his potential could be when he tried at all. We had a moment of calm in a very large storm.

I dropped him off at his first AA meeting and watched him walk in, wondering if maybe it was going to be all right. We had found a solution. He came out with a small white disc in his hand—his first AA chip. And he had the name of a sponsor who he called all the time. Things were coming together. I could not only go back to writing, but I could put together what Louie would need for his next adventure. Graduation, then college beckoned. There were still fences to be mended with people he had disappointed, but all of that would come.

At all of the graduation events and awards ceremonies I watched Louie from afar and the old thought came back. How much of this did I cause? He seemed uncomfortable in his own skin, twitchy, and ready to have it all over with. At his confirmation in church five years earlier, the last big milestone he had in a group, he was more relaxed and smiling. The entire extended family had been there back then. Granddaddy had come to see his first grandchild be confirmed in the same faith he had devoted his life to serving. He had been the minister who baptized Louie.

I was the only family member at all of the extra events surrounding graduation from high school. Louie had found it easier to be alone or among people who didn't ask too many questions or bring up Grand-daddy's name. Occasionally, I still tried, testing the waters, as much to have my father live again in a memory as to see if Louie was healing at all.

"What are you doing?" was his usual response and the conversations always dropped off.

Now, I walked into the school auditorium for the next awards cere-mony feeling a little uneasy. Not the right emotion for the beginning of my son's graduation week. Some sense of relief, no euphoria.

Hundreds of parents dutifully filed in to the Godwin High School gym doing a wobbly high-step up the bleachers to find a seat. We waited for the senior awards ceremony to begin, packed in tight, knees wide around the shoulders of the person in front of us. I made polite small talk with the nice pharmacist next to me. This was his second go-round. He had a daughter graduate last year. He was comfortably relaxed, explaining to me that we had three hours of sitting on the narrow wooden bench before this would all be over. Over.

I had done my best to help Louie, encouraging him, and for a little while it was working, but with the addition of alcohol it was all a slip-pery slope just a short distance away from collapse. Sitting there, I didn't want to admit it, so I focused on Louie.

Here I sat in the bleachers, watching him walk in wearing the red cap and gown—the only one doing a triumphant swagger—as he turned and gave me the thumbs up. The nice pharmacist chuckled and nudged me. I tried not to fast-forward in my head to August. In a couple of months, Louie was heading off to Marshall University in West Vir-ginia, his father's alma mater.

He took off his mortarboard and rubbed his hair, looking around. He wasn't happy. It was all an outward act. But we were here. We had made it. Eighteen years of struggling with school, and the big day was here.

Graduation came on a hot June day. I was wearing a new outfit sit-ting alongside Louie in his red cap and gown as he drove in bumper-to-bumper traffic to the Segal Center where almost every school in the area was holding their graduation in shifts. We watched students wearing dark blue gowns who had just graduated walk in droves down the sidewalk in one direction while kids in red gowns for the next ceremony were getting out of cars and hoofing it to make it in time for their line-up.

Louie was dying to smoke a cigarette, another confession he had made recently. Normally, I would have made speeches and pointed out all the reasons for not smoking, but I had given up a lot of ground and just told him he had to wait until I was out of the car. It was making the tension worse.

"You sure you don't want to get out and walk? I can park the car," I said.

"No, we're fine. Stop." Stop talking, he meant.

I was wound a little tight. This was the end of something. Something was over, the thought occurred time and again. And it wasn't happening with a fanfare but a sigh of exhausted relief. Not exactly how I'd pictured the moment.

We couldn't get to that parking garage fast enough so that I could walk on ahead and Louie could light up and get in one long drag before he went to join his friends.

I was by myself. Some family members were somewhere else in the large arena, but I didn't know where. His father was in prison, but his stepmother was somewhere in the crowd, and his father had managed to get through by phone to wish Louie a good day. I found a seat in front, squeezing on the end of a row, and waited for the procession to start.

At long last, Louie came marching in along with his best friends I had known since they started in kindergarten together. His special education teacher, Bonnie Thompson, who had guided him through the past two years, was sitting nearby in her cap and gown and gave me a smile and a wave. I waved back before turning my head, not wanting to cry and not sure if I was crying from joy or sadness.

Louie strode up to the side of the stage, waiting for his turn to cross over to a new beginning. As he got his diploma he hugged everyone enthusiastically, enveloping his small principal, Debra Bishop, in a wave of shiny, red nylon.

This is a truth I have come to learn about long dark passages in life. There are still moments of joy that can reach opposite points to the measure of sadness that is being endured, at the same time. It is possible to reach out and feel both. Louie was in one of those moments. I was not.

I was living through the moment, trying my best to absorb the happiness that was there and finding it harder and harder to get past all of it. I kept a tight smile across my face, but inside I was wondering if Louie was going to make it.

That night we went to a graduation party at his best friend's house. My brother and his family were there, and we all sat around listening to speeches. Louie and his friends left to go to a few graduation parties at friends' houses.

"Bye, Mom. I'll see you around three," he said, giving me a hug as he left.

That night he drank himself into oblivion again, breaking the short fragile sobriety we had captured for a little while.

This is where hell began. Every nicety we may have tried to plaster over things to get through another day crumbled. Neither one of us had the will or the strength to try anymore.

Louie stopped going to meetings, stopped coming home at night, stopped trying to hide any corner of the anger about losing his grandfather, losing his home, losing the rest of his family that he had been living with for so long.

"The only reason I drink is because of you," he spit out one night, before he drove off in a squeal of tires, disappearing until well into the next day.

"We live in a ghetto. You're just poor white trash," he said another time in the brief glimpses I got of him that let me know he was still alive. "When I leave here for college I'm never coming back. I will never come back to this house again. I cannot wait to leave here. This is hell."

It was his favorite mantra. That and occasionally threatening suicide as a means to get me to do something for him, or at least back off.

I stopped writing. I stopped doing much of anything and started counting the days till he was off to college. I didn't have the will to push him out, and he had burned the bridges with everyone else except for those he could drink with till late in the night, playing poker at a house in a fancy subdivision nearby. Louie used that like a weapon, comparing the townhouse we rented to those fancy brick digs with a pool in the back. It took all the restraint I had not to stand on their front lawn and scream out in anger about how they were making it easier for my son to disappear into an alcoholic haze.

I knew it wasn't the whole truth. If he wasn't there, it would have been someplace else. At least this way, I had some clue about where he was driving off to when he'd leave in a tide of angry words.

This went on for weeks and got gradually worse by degrees. Louie had lost every job he ever had and only showed up on occasion to tell me about how much nicer, how much better every other family was that he came into contact with, and anyone else who was letting him sleep off the drunks. I listened benignly, relieved to know he'd made it through one more day.

I started to feel like I was going crazy. Money became even tighter. I wasn't doing much beyond taking long walks. I sold one of the cars and the fold-out couch and ottoman in his room to pay the bills. We were both sliding away. I was trying to hold on and was selling what I could, thinking Louie was only weeks away from leaving. But he took it as another mark against my character and stayed away for longer stretches. Maybe he was right.

"If I didn't need a ride to college, I'd already be gone," he said, before he left to say goodbye to all of his friends. When he came back to sleep off another long night I found a case of beer and an open bottle of vodka in the back of the car. I threw it away in the nearest trash can, telling Louie I did.

"I don't know how it got there," he says. I didn't bother to answer him. We'd sunk to the level of the ridiculous.

Finally, the day came to drive him to Marshall. "Did you pack for me?" he snarled from the couch in the living room. He had returned some time in the night.

I hadn't done a thing for him. I was done. This six-hour drive ahead of us was going to be my last act.

He scooped everything up at the last minute into large green garbage bags and stuffed it all into the back of the car. We took turns driving. Just sitting next to him quietly was enough to send him off into a litany about how I had failed, what I had done wrong, and why he was so glad to be leaving me behind.

I looked at him blankly, trying to get through the ride, and he'd scream, "Do something! Show some emotion!"

I was done and I knew better than to take the bait. It was like being trapped in a burlap bag with an angry cat, claws bared. I didn't ask any questions, didn't start any conversations, and did my best not to react to any comments.

My father's death, his sudden absence, felt like another lifetime. The Louie I had once known was a completely different person. I had stopped thinking about him in terms of when he might come back. Instead, I was grieving what had left forever, and I wasn't interested in getting to know this Louie. We couldn't get to Marshall University fast enough, and we didn't stop for anything but gas, driving up into the green mountains of West Virginia.

We finally got there, late as it turned out, and I interrupted a meeting of the new resident advisors to get someone to give us a key to Louie's room.

"Don't, stop," Louie said behind me, but I was determined to get this done. Over.

One of his friends from Richmond found us, followed closely behind by his brother and parents. It was one of his drinking buddies. It was a surreal moment making small talk with the parents like it was a great day, a launching of their lives.

Louie chatted and helped carry things. He was civil for the entire half hour they were with us. The moment they left he turned to me and said, "We can do this nicely or I can just walk away. Which one do you want?"

I knew what he was saying. If I tried to hang around for a moment longer or take part in any of the parent functions on campus, he was going to walk away from me now and not look back. Or, I could get a perfunctory hug and leave now. I took the hug.

On the drive back I rode with all of the windows down, the cool mountain air blasting through the car. I felt free again.

Back at the house I found old beer cans lined up in his room as a last nasty finger gesture in my direction. Empty beer boxes were pushed into his closet where he knew I'd find them, and bottle caps were everywhere. It was all assembled for my benefit. But, I was beyond caring and too far into being unmoored from what I had thought was important. I was slipping away.

At long last, I showed up at an Al-Anon meeting and unloaded. A circle of people took me in and by then, I was a sight. Barely sleeping, barely eating.

Afterward, a woman came up to me, smiling. "When you're married to it, you can blame their mother, but then you go and raise an alcoholic and it bites you in the ass," she said. Others told me snippets of their stories afterward.

I had tripped into my own secret garden that held the magic I was going to need to get further down the path and let go, forever. Fortunately, hell was coming to an end, but not without a few last twists. And the last home I was to visit was going to hold the key to all of it, finally giving me the last of my answer and making me forever grateful I took a chance and set out on the journey. Mercy happened.

Chapter 5

Finding Mercy

The story of the Mercy Home for Boys & Girls, Chicago, Illinois, founded in 1887 by Father Louis Campbell as St. Paul's Home for Working Boys

EDDIE'S STORY

> *"Far better to dare mighty things, to win glorious triumphs, even though checkered by failure, than to take rank with those poor spirits who neither enjoy much nor suffer much . . . in the grey twilight that knows not victory nor defeat."*
>
> **Teddy Roosevelt**

*E*ddie Gamble left home at fourteen, choosing the streets of the south side of Chicago over home in Cabrini Green, one of the most famous and notorious public housing projects in the country. "I was fighting with my stepfather. My mother wanted to be with him, I didn't and she chose him." His mother told the boy she was going to be with her boyfriend and her son couldn't return. His biological father had left two years prior to that.

"He was an evil, evil man," Eddie says, and it is all he says. We leave the memories of the stepfather behind and move on to what it was like for a young teenager to try and get by on the city streets by himself.

"I spent about two years on the streets, very rough. You don't have food, you don't have shelter, you don't have clothes, you don't know where you're going to be from day to day. I borrowed money. I stole food. I slept on trains and rooftops and curled up in chairs. I still had friends in Cabrini Green and could go by there for food."

While on the streets he enrolled himself in Chicago's alternative school for students who have been kicked out of the regular public schools or dropped out to make up credits before returning to regular, accredited schools. The school never realized he was homeless. "Never came up. I had two sets of clothes and a friend. She'd wash the clothes I wasn't wearing, for me."

While visiting a friend at Cabrini Green, a juvenile probation officer came by and Eddie reached out, asking if she knew of any place that might take Eddie in and give him the support he needed. He was determined to make something more of himself than what the world was currently offering. She told him about Mercy.

"Mercy Boys Home wasn't the same as it is now," said Eddie. "Back then, if they interviewed you and found out your situation, they let you move in and then they'd talk to you," he said, referring to the week-long process of testing and evaluations that go on now.

His favorite memory of Mercy is his first day. "When I first got there, I just stood there and looked at the room. I just wanted to lay down and rest. I didn't have to worry about anyone going through my pockets or getting in a fight with someone," he said. "It was the first time I had slept in a bed in two years.

Mercy stepped in and did everything a family is supposed to do, he said, including creating a sense of belonging and nurturing. "Father Close gave me good advice, gave me a sense of self. They created that family atmosphere, truly. It was everything that I needed when I needed it."

Twelve years ago, when he married his wife, Maurya, Father Close performed the ceremony. Now, he has three children: Mya, eleven; Elias, eight; and Ethan, four. "Life for my children will be different, and that's by design," he said.

Now, Eddie works as an investigator for the Illinois Attorney General's office and goes back to Mercy to give motivational speeches and stay in touch with the people who are his family.

"They saved me, gave me the support I was looking for: food, shelter, school. I can not possibly give back everything that I have gotten. If you're ready to do something with yourself and you need a support system, I think that's what they provide.

"I'll be singing their praises long before I'm gone and I'll leave it in the will to sing their praises after I'm gone."

> *"What lies behind us and what lies before us are tiny matters compared to what lies within us."*
>
> **Ralph Waldo Emerson**

*M*ercy Home is a residential education facility run by the archdiocese as a Catholic charity, one of the healthiest Catholic charities in the country, with two campuses—one for boys and one for girls—in the heart of the city of Chicago. Every home may want to be able to do that but Mercy can, and it all began with a fable.

During the Depression there were several Catholic orphanages around the Chicago area. Each neighborhood had its own, taking care of the nearby population—except for Mercy. Mercy took in all of the children no one else wanted.

Father Kelly, who ran the home at the time, turned to the other Catholic homes around Chicago and asked for financial assistance from each of them to help the children who came from all of those neighborhoods. But he was rejected by all of them, as they claimed financial insecurity.

Father Kelly contacted parish priests across the country and asked them to send their local white pages. He then had the children of Mercy call everyone with Catholic-sounding names and ask them for a donation. It was religious arm-twisting that worked like a charm.

Today grandchildren of the original contributors still donate to the bottom line. "The small donors are the backbone," said Mark Schmeltzer, director of communications. The other homes around Chicago that refused to help have long since closed their doors and faded away.

Ninety-seven percent of the cost of Mercy Home is underwritten by the Catholic Church and private donations. Parents, who for the most part are from the surrounding low-income neighborhoods of Chicago, pay an amount on a sliding scale. The fee, which can be as little as ten dollars, is mostly symbolic to keep the surrounding family members involved and invested. Mercy never takes its focus off of the goal of rebuilding the entire family back into a sustainable, functioning whole.

The older campus, the Hay campus for boys, is west of the loop in Chicago, and the girl's campus is on the old Walgreen estate in the Beverly and Morgan Park area of south Chicago. The boys' campus is made up of four main buildings stretching across a city block. Going from east to west, there's a big indoor soccer building on Adam and Aberdeen Streets, followed by a one-story office building and then the Father Close Home on Adams, which has three floors and contains eight of the home programs for boys. The old original building from the orphanage's early days now houses the president's office, the cafeteria, Kelly Home, and the old Mission Press. In the early days the boys of Mercy Home put out a newspaper and were known colloquially as "Father Kelly's Newsboys." The three main buildings are all connected by short hallways and staircases that were added as afterthoughts, making navigation a little confusing for people new to the campus. Eighty boys and young men from the ages of eleven to the early twenties live in the homes. They must agree to stay at least one full year.

The girls' campus on the old Walgreen estate is along what was once one of the poshest streets in south Chicago. It sits side-by-side with other historical and stately mansions that are so inspiring. Carl Sandburg once wrote a poem about the neighborhood called, "Beverly Hill, Chicago." Forty-two girls can stay in the programs at Mercy, and both campuses are generally always at capacity.

Mercy describes their mission as "serving the poor in spirit," but only with their willing participation. That caveat makes them unique.

The journey to a residential education facility sometimes has more to do with waning choices and typically begins with a judge ordering a child removed from the custody of parents and placed in foster care. Sometimes the cause is neglect, sometimes abuse, and, more often these days, drugs and alcohol are involved—the parent's addictions, not the child's. Through no fault of his own, a child finds himself moved to unfamiliar surroundings with no input into how long he might stay or where he might go next.

The choices that are left have become uncertain, malleable, and are in the shifting hands of professionals, not the families.

Many times the first foster placements don't work out and the child finds himself packing up the few belongings that are the touchstone to a home he once had and moving on to yet another house, another situation.

Eventually, trust ebbs away and, still attached legally to absent parents, the child is placed in a residential education facility that can offer the psychological counseling that has become necessary, maybe even vital.

But that's not the path to Mercy.

"We are able to partner with families so children can return home," said Dan King, Donor Relations Manager for Mercy Home. At Mercy, he said, they talk about "roots and wings." There are two main goals at Mercy, which is supported by Catholic Charities, the foremost benefactor of orphanages worldwide.

The first goal is to give a sense of rootedness to the child and to the parents and build a confidence within that will foster the derring-do it takes to use their wings and set out. The second is to restore the child to his original family and work to restore every member, not just the child, through mentoring and classes for both parents and children.

Parents who are young or overwhelmed, or older grandparents who cannot cope with raising a grandchild, are encouraged to come in and seek help before things get out of hand. A plan is devised to help everyone strengthen their skills and get a better idea of where they're going and how to get there.

Almost without exception, no one who comes to Mercy has been through the foster care system first and bounced around. No one has gathered the anger and frustration of getting to know one place only to wake up in a new situation, with a new set of rules, a new schedule to learn.

"The only way we'd get a kid who'd gone through multiple placements is if he was a ward of the state," said King. And they don't take in many of those.

In other words, either the child has a family around him, or the ties have already been permanently severed. At Mercy there is no hazy middle ground like other residential facilities that accept children from social services on a regular basis. "We're trying to form a partnership with the parents," said Brother Brian Maloney, manager of the admissions department.

No child is returned to a parent who has failed multiple drug tests, but still retains their rights, or has a history of abuse but has made repeated pledges to change. The opposite is a common occurrence for children in the welfare system, according to the Pew Report on Children in Foster Care a leading study of the failures of the foster care system in America.

The child knows if he chooses to enter Mercy how long he'll be staying and where he's headed after that. The home asks each child and custodial parent to agree to a one-year commitment, which can be extended. Even though the child is a minor, his agreement is a factor in being accepted at Mercy Home.

After their stay at Mercy most of the children will go back home. For some it will be going out into the wider world after graduating from high school. And most do graduate and go on to college. Mercy often pays college tuition and in 2006 had twenty-five children in college and two young ladies in post-graduate schools.

The children of Mercy retain a sense of control. It's a necessary ingredient in adulthood to avoid feeling like a permanent victim and to make choices later to build an independent, happy life. The home does not assume guardianship of any child.

A more typical experience for a child caught in the child welfare system is to understand that this room in a foster home is theirs, for now, and these people, the foster parents, will be their guardians, for now. The equivalent for an adult would be having a job and an apartment, but with the caveat that the company is thinking about laying off employees and the apartment is about to go condo. It's hard to focus on building a solid foundation, getting good grades, and planning for college, if the basics are always up in the air.

Mercy escapes the issue of children being suddenly moved around by the courts by focusing on private placements. The government never gets involved, although social workers and judges quite often recommend Mercy to families in trouble but haven't quite fallen into the system.

In another trend away from most modern residential education facilities that have adopted the use of individual cottages with "teaching parents," children live in a dorm and dining hall setting—a group setting with a wider definition of family. The boys dormitories are set in what looks like modern condos with a vista of the Chicago skyline, and the boys have been known to say to new friends from school, "Do you want to see my condo?"

The winding hall and stairways of the boys' campus have displays

Doing homework in one of the "condos" with a view.

of various moments in Mercy history and a lot of aqua green paint. It was apparently a favorite color of Father James Close, who retired after 33 years and in 2006 was replaced by Father Scott Donahue, the eighth president of Mercy and the eighth Irishman. The color is an eye-catcher and is on all of the trim and the fabled front door—the large, heavy wooden oak door that has been there since 1909, still attached to the old building. Mark Schmeltzer, a Chicago native, has familial attachments to the door, like a lot of residents of the city.

His father, Fred, who is now seventy-one years old, was sent by his mother, Dorothy, every year as a teenager to drop off old toys during the holidays and knock on the door. "He had to ride the streetcar in winter, a long ride. I brought him back to see it earlier this year," said Mark. "I brought him back to see the other side of the door where the nuns came to get the toys. It made him think about his mom and what a great lady she was."

The door is so famous that its image is used in a lot of Mercy materials as an instantly recognized symbol—even with the added sea of green.

All of the renovations, including the recently completed five-year expansion, have grown off of this building snaking around the property, expanding outwards from *the door.*

Across town at the old Walgreen estate, which looks like something from an old-style Hollywood set, is the girls' campus donated in the late 1950s to the Catholic Church. It had been a retreat home for the Sisters of the Senacle until 1986 when it was put up for sale for $750,000. Father Close made a phone call to Charles Walgreen who purchased the property back and donated it to the home, allowing them to admit girls beginning in 1987 in time for the home's centennial celebration. It's now known as the Walgreen campus.

The two campuses mix a couple of times every year including the academic banquet, a picnic at the girls' campus, a popular talent show, community service, and several Christmas events.

The girls' campus at the Mercy Home for Boys and Girls.

Between the two campuses there are fourteen programs, labeled "homes" by Mercy, with different structures to fit the different age groups, genders, and needs. Kids range in age from eleven to their early twenties and sleep two to a room. All of the children attend school off-campus at a variety of private and public schools. Counselors do their best to match every child with the school best suited to their needs.

Every child who shows up on Mercy's doorstep is given assistance, even if it's determined there is another home that would be a better fit. No one is turned away who wants help, said Brother Brian Maloney. "We never have a fully closed case if you will," he said. "That's why the administrative process starts as soon as we pick up the phone," said Juan Medina, director of admissions, and goes on for seven days with testing and evaluations. These children have already faced too many letdowns and they want to be sure it's a good fit before admitting someone into one of the homes.

However, if it's necessary to refer someone elsewhere, Mercy makes the phone calls looking for the right place and availability before passing on the information. "If we do give referrals and they don't work, we tell them to call us and come back in and we'll try to find the right place," said Brother Brian. "We will provide care to anyone who knocks on our door. It's God's mercy in action."

"Typically what happens," says Tita Yutuc, vice-president of youth programs and a veteran of the home at nineteen years, "is a teacher says, 'I have a couple of kids in my class' and they'll talk to them and suggest they talk to Mercy. The highest level of referrals we receive are from the Chicago Public School System. We've had homeless kids, we've had kids close to eighteen.... [We had a case where] one parent was an alcoholic, one was mentally ill. We went out and looked for the parents, who wouldn't sign them in. So, we said, this is where they are if you want them."

The children, two boys in their teens, had never had a place to call home before. "I'll never forget that moment," said Tita. "They were carrying their boxes. The elevator was broken and they had to walk and not one of them was complaining because they've never had a home before." They walked into their new rooms in awe and sat down, taking it all in. They finally had a place to call home.

The move toward more social services and outreach began under Father Close and followed the national trend of residential education and foster care.

Milieu Therapy, which uses peer discussion and resolution aided by a therapist, was added along with therapists on campus where they could be seen as part of the extended family instead of in a pre-arranged office setting for just an hour. The service is available to any Mercy child who is in need of counseling.

As part of the therapy nightly meetings are held with the program manager, therapists, and advocates of the home to discuss how the day went, ways to make things better, and to generally check in with each resident.

In Cooke Home, for boys from fourteen to sixteen, there is a Milieu meeting going on, and two of the boys are interested in moving up a level to earn more privileges. In order for that to happen the two boys have to ask the other boys in the Cooke Home program for their insight and a group vote is then taken. Cornelius, a resident of Cooke, speaks up, carefully assessing the strengths of each candidate, praising them for changes they've made in their behavior and recommending them for the upgrade with the advice to "keep doing what you're doing, so you don't go back."

What's most remarkable about the exchange is that Cornelius has schizophrenia, and when he arrived at Mercy, from a supportive intact family, he was aggressive, never made eye-contact, and required on-site schooling. Now his social skills are smooth, mature and empowering not only to the boys he is addressing by looking at them directly, but for himself. It is evidence of Brother Maloney's assertion that all things are possible at Mercy.

Over at the girls' campus on the Walgreen estate, another Milieu meeting is taking place among the girls of the Couderc Home, led by Monti Clayton, their fifty-two-year-old program manager who has been there since 1989. The girls are older, more contemplative than an earlier meeting for the Seton Home girls where the younger participants had to be admonished to keep both feet on the ground, sit up, and pay attention.

At Seton Home, the girls are for the most part sitting up straight along matching maroon couches and love seats in an oversized family room. Along one wall is a bookcase filled with games. Stuffed teddy bears are on top.

Linda Hendrickson, twenty-nine years old, is the program manager for Seton, which has nine girls between eleven and fourteen. Anna Lise is their therapist. The state of Illinois requires that all licensed homes for girls in the state have only female workers. The rule doesn't apply to boys.

The girls are discussing the annual Christmas Wish List, which applies to both campuses. Each child gets to write down three desires,

A lounge in one of the girls' residential homes.

each not costing more than fifty dollars. It's a hot topic, just like it was over in boys' Cooke home, but with different desires. Fewer electronics, more clothes.

After the meeting, Daria, who is fourteen, in the eighth grade, and has been here two months comes over to chat. She sits down next to me and tells me a little about her life in free form, letting the words flow.

"When you first get here you have a lot of issues, a lot of confrontations, but I knew I couldn't because I read the manual," she says. Each child who enters Mercy is given a manual that spells out the basic rules and lets them know what to expect. "Eighth grade is a little hard. I'm in private school, it's very new, hard for me to keep my focus. I stay up with my work, stay focused; if I'm having trouble I raise my hand.

"I have an ABC plan. A: finish law school and be a lawyer; B: love music, become a singer or dancer."

"She is a good dancer," says another of the girls hanging out on a nearby couch. Daria smiles and continues laying out her plan.

"C: be a good mom and finish all my dreams that I want. I want to visit a lot of places. If I have a lot of money I want to visit Paris and live in Paris with my nice husband and have twin girls and twin boys. I always wanted a twin. Someone to dress alike with and someone to talk with," she says, winding down.

Julia, a serious girl at thirteen with glasses and deep dimples, who has been here a little longer at three months, settles in next to me to tell her story. She is soft spoken and determined. These aren't conversations as much as requests to witness what has been and what might be. It's what happens when there is so much change in a short amount of time. You just want someone to know you're still here.

The conversation with her dips and turns a little and I remain quiet, letting her get it out. It takes no prompting.

"It's hard at first," she says, "to get used to it. I'm the artist. I've been thinking about being a cartoonist, also about being a veterinarian. When you first start out here you don't know what to do," she says,

A meeting at the Mercy Home.

bouncing back and forth between topics. "There are so many rules. I'm actually getting better grades. I'm in a better school. This school that I'm at now is just a lot easier. Adjusting to school was easy; being the new girl was hard. I was a C, D, and F person. I've only been there a couple of months and now I'm getting Cs and Bs."

Dinner is brought up to the Seton home from a general kitchen. Over at the girls' campus dinner is served family-style in each individual home, and the girls trot off to help out. We eat a hot chicken dish together at small circular tables, chatting about the day.

Back over in the Couderc Milieu meeting, a young girl from Seton is visiting. Neiva is ready to move up to Couderc, but it means leaving her best friend and roommate behind. Moving up always means changing programs and moving to a different part of the campus. A child can apply to change levels or the recommendation can come from a staff member. The decision is made by the home managers, the child involved, and with input from the members of her potential new home. She is tentative with very wide eyes, arms crossed protectively in front of her, and she speaks only in whispers, if at all.

The topic for the meeting is gossip, a good one for girls. The girls are all open and honest about their own motivations, owning up to their mistakes, their desires.

Another young woman, Sandra, works at making a connection with Neiva. She talks openly and easily with the group about trust and people coming into their own strengths, deciding for themselves who they should be.

"They respect us, we respect them," says Monti. "They tell me their ideas and I try to incorporate them." A recent big success was an all-night movie night with popcorn.

Father Close began the trend toward creating a family atmosphere at Mercy that meant children should always be heard, appreciated, respected, and loved. Okpara Rice, the director of residential programs for the boys' Hay Campus, is a part of the new order at Mercy that gives more of an emphasis on creating a family atmosphere for the children. The old way of doing things emphasized hard work and education with very little therapeutic input.

"You're given a responsibility to shape young men's lives and that's an honor," he said.

Okpara, married to Julie and new father to Malcolm (whose smiling face peers out of frames on the shelves behind him) is easy-going and confident, which belies his beginnings. He can appreciate and understand what the boys under his care are going through, because he comes from the same background.

"I'm the son of a drug addict who lost everything and ended up homeless. You just make do," said Okpara, who grew up on the south side of Chicago. "It's a horrible way to live, I can tell you that. School is not a priority, survival is a priority. But you don't have to live that kind of life," he continued.

New residents have a hard time believing they can learn to enjoy life and school, but it's necessary to begin to invest in their own lives. Okpara was unaware of Mercy Home but was blessed with a mother and grandmother who believed in him and told him he could do it. He kept going, earned his GED, and went on to Loyola University Chicago, eventually earning a masters degree in social work.

What he took away from his early life was not only the empathy for every child with a hard beginning, but the gift of his early role models. Everyone needs someone to believe in them and to tell them so, often. "They need to know that you can be a success," he said. Although his office is not near the boys' living area, he makes a point of going over to them and getting involved, rather than just reading the reports from the program managers of each home. "It's my duty to know the kids," he said.

Boscoe Home, which is for boys eleven to seventeen, presents the most challenges, has the highest number of at-risk residents and the most restrictions. Initial placements of children in each home are determined through extensive testing that takes place over the course of a few days. After that, staff gets together to decide if Mercy can help the child and where the appropriate spot might be found to place them. The Boscoe program is very incentive-based with rewards such as "Youth of the Month." "These are not bad kids," says Okpara. "They may get that at home or in school, but they aren't seen that way here." To tease their counselors the boys of Boscoe Home created "Employee of the Hall." Like all of the boys' homes but one, there is a point system in place with points being rewarded for good behavior or good grades, which also helps when it comes time to move to a different level and more privileges.

Children tend to model what adults present to them. Call a child bad or unwanted often enough, and don't be surprised if he starts to buy into it and become that. But, it also means the opposite is true. Appeal to the best part of anyone, nurture what you want to see, and that will take root and blossom. Louie was like this.

Every year Louie had at least one teacher who didn't want to deal with somebody who had learning disabilities and took it out on Louie, trying to push him out of the room for not being able to follow the directions the first go-round or for not hearing the order to "quiet down" the first time. It's a way of trying to make the child responsible for how the adult feels, rather than the adult looking out for each child.

But, I also knew when Louie had found a teacher who was empowering him without him saying anything to me. He would start spouting information on one topic, like earth science or World War II, completely engrossed in the facts, and his grade would bounce upwards. In other words, Louie always gave back what he was receiving, pouring out more of what was given to him—bad or good. Every place he felt he was being respected for who he was, rather than torn down, Louie responded by opening up and learning. That's the legacy Okpara is passing on from his grandmother and mother to all of these children.

The Speh and Noah Homes are where the youngest boys reside, eleven to fourteen years old, and they require the most hands-on time, the most patience, Okpara told me. "They have the funniest sense of humor," he said. "They want to play, to get out. In the morning, they're ready to go. They need that attention."

Not everyone can work with this age group. Imagine having eight boys who all want you to see their latest success or share a joke with you or tell a long story about school. Now combine that with a background that includes neglect or abuse with a lack of basic skills. "They'll wear you out," said Okpara.

"To do this you have got to love them. There was a boy in Noah whose whole family has been horribly sexually abused and knowing what he's dealing with in therapy and watching him deal with his issues—we've got to appreciate what they're going through. If you don't then it's just numbers and budgets."

The Daley Home, for boys from eleven to seventeen, is the least restrictive and is the only one that doesn't have a point system. Unlike the other cottages where the boys work on moving from a more restrictive environment to a lesser one, Daley Home works with a more natural family order. In Daley there are fewer behavioral issues, and therapy is an option rather than a requirement. The kids tend to be with each other longer and look out for each other more. Many of these children come to Mercy from a family that can no longer care for them rather than because of issues such as neglect, abuse or addictions.

Sheil and Campbell Homes are for boys from sixteen to eighteen years old who are learning to be independent young men. There is no one telling them when to get up or where they need to be, and there is more planning going on for the life that awaits them out there.

"A lot of the guys . . . they're motivated. They really want to get their lives together. They struggle, they leave gangs behind," said Okpara. "There's more turnover in kids there. We had a kid leave Sheil Home and come back in three days. His stepfather was drinking and the kid shows up at night with his stuff and wanted to come back," he said. When kids abruptly leave, their beds are left open for seven days just in case the reality outside wasn't what they had thought it would be.

"He had wanted to be home to help. He knew where he came from, a family of drug abusers, but he was close to his grandmother and he wanted to be there to help her," he said. "There's this pull from both worlds and you have to make that okay for them. They're so resilient." The young man was about to move up from Sheil Home, onto Kelly Home where there are fewer restrictions and more responsibilities.

Recently, a young man's father showed up at one of the homes, high on drugs and asking the son for money. The son paid his father to go away. He wasn't embarrassed; he knew everyone there had similar experiences. There was no teasing.

The boys of Cooke and Mahoney, the young teenagers, are freshmen and sophomores just emerging out of puberty. "These guys, hands down, you spend a lot of time with, disciplinary-wise," said Okpara.

"Guy came through the door toying with gangs, father in prison," he said, beginning another story that illustrates the point that a young teenage boy will find trouble if he's determined. "He went AWOL from school one day. We got a call from the school—he'd been shot. First time in my career I got that call. I couldn't find his mom. He was shot in the back while running away by a kid on a bike. Petty. He should have been at school.

"I remember standing next to his bed and him coming out of it and I could tell he was tough and how afraid he was. He hasn't learned his lesson yet, but he's better. I understand his mindset. It's the fantasy." The child wants to believe that his home life will magically repair itself.

This is the age where therapy becomes more focused and intense to deal with the harder issues—the muck, Okpara calls it—so that the boys can leave some of the baggage of the past behind them when they eventually leave Mercy.

"Such hard work that they do," he said. "Hitting it every day with enthusiasm and energy."

Jobs become a part of the program as well. Younger boys earn an allowance of ten to fifteen dollars per week. Regardless of age, all of the basic needs are met at Mercy, without exception. Every child who comes to Mercy can finally stop wondering about where the next meal or new pair of shoes is coming from. When Okpara sees a need, he knows he can easily fill it. No child goes without. "That's what keeps me extending my time here. You go home feeling like, wow, you really did help somebody today."

One of the ways Mercy stands out among other homes is its powerful fund-raising that makes all of these vast programs possible. They have a powerful direct mail campaign along with strong corporate support, and it shows in what they're able to more easily do for all of their residents than other residential education facilities. If a child needs braces for their teeth, it's provided. If a resident works hard, gets great grades, and is accepted into Harvard, Mercy foots the bill. Not too long ago a resident needed chemotherapy and Mercy made sure it was taken care of.

Several large fund-raising events help out with Mercy's mission and budget. The most popular of them is Ringside for Mercy's Sake, started by Pat Arbor, a former resident of Mercy and former chairman of the Chicago Board of Trade, and Jack Sandner, a former Golden Glove and Catholic Youth Organization (CYO) fighter, friend of Pat Arbor, and former chairman of the Chicago Mercantile Exchange. Ringside for Mercy's Sake is about to celebrate its fifteenth year with eight bouts between traders and brokers from the Chicago exchanges as boxers. Some are amateurs, some have participated in Golden Gloves, and "some are just tough guys," said Mark Schmeltzer, director of communications.

Glenn Leonard, forty-nine, who fought in the first Ringside and won easily even though he was coming straight off a plane from Jamaica, now recruits and trains potential fighters. Originally with the Chicago Board of Trades for twenty-three years, Glenn wanted to open his own gym and made a deal with the home in 2003 to use some of their space to open the West Loop Conditioning Club. He operated the gym in exchange for training fighters for the big night.

It had an unexpected bonus when he met his wife MaryAnne, who works for Mercy in special events like Ringside. They've been married now for six years. It's not uncommon for single Mercy employees to find their mate on the job. Mark Schmeltzer met Kelly Lee, who does the assessments at Mercy for kids just entering the home. Their wedding is planned for sometime in the spring of 2008. They make a good match. She laughs easily at all of his jokes, and he wisely checks with her before giving any answers about the wedding.

Right outside of Mark's office there are piles of prizes being sorted through by staff and volunteers. The 2006 Ringside includes a silent auction with a lot of sports memorabilia and a raffle of a 2007 Jaguar XJ convertible.

Also on the Hay campus is the 20/30 Club located near the gym and marked by a green neon sign at the entrance. It was formed by a volunteer group of men in their early twenties and thirties who wanted to put on special events to benefit the home such as the Hoops to Homework program. Boys within the home, with a wide range of skills, form basketball teams to play each other. The catch is they must maintain their homework and their grades. The season lasts throughout the winter months, which in Chicago can start to seem a little long, and into the spring and is very popular.

"Back in the 1980s we laid the foundation for a number of these programs under Father Close, to make Mercy the best of its kind in the country," said Mark Mroz, vice-president of agency advancement, who came to the home from Chicago's city hall where he worked in the mayor's office.

"When I came [to Mercy] Father Close asked me to do three things: increase public relations in Chicago; form a board of advisors made up of city, business, civic, and philanthropic people to help raise money and be involved in the home; and pull together special events. At that point, they were primarily raising money through the mail," Mroz said.

Father Close also saw as far back as the eighties that the family structure needed to be replicated for former Mercy residents after they were gone. Being able to call someone for advice or knowing there was somebody out there who would always listen was just as essential as the day-to-day care provided to the younger boys. "Previously the father had the idea that once you left, you didn't come back. This was your history," said Daniel Nelson, the enthusiastic twenty-seven-year-old program manager for AfterCare. But once the dynamic was changed, more and more started coming back, seeking advice and help.

Programs and homes were assembled for older kids and alumni, creating a far-reaching and effective aftercare program. The cost for residents in the two AfterCare homes is around $21,000 per young man every year. Potential residents are asked to make a commitment of at least one year before they enter. Kelly Home was created for young men who still need some structure or wrap-around care and offers a variety of life skills, such as classes on budgeting, insurance, and credit. Regular assessments are done quarterly, at which time the young man may move up to Quill Home where the skills they've learned in Kelly Home will be demonstrated and applied.

Quill Home, which began at an off-campus site on Chicago's north side, is the most independent living facility at Mercy. It's where the young men prepare for the transition to adulthood. Both were added for young men eighteen and older and are unique because they offer longer-term care than other homes. The residents go to college nearby, often Malcolm X or Daley Community College, and hold down jobs while paying a small rent to the home that is returned in the form of a savings account when they leave and go out on their own. As an after-thought, Brother Maloney mentioned that the program has been known to admit young men who are adults but still have a few things to learn. They remain flexible to better serve the community.

≈≈)(≈≈

I thought of Louie for a moment, but put the thought aside. He was ensconced at Marshall University in his own version of happiness. I knew he wouldn't budge. However, things were already going badly for him. After a brief, alcohol-filled honeymoon phase, he had gotten arrested, on my birthday, September 6, for being in possession of alcohol in public, throwing a chair through a window, and fleeing on foot. He was in the company of a fraternity that wanted to pledge him but had left him high and dry when the police showed up. He was the only one who was caught, arrested, and jailed overnight. His hands were bloody from being tackled in the glass, and he was pretty banged up.

That's where our lives had gotten to. He called me the next day to tell me what had happened and to ask for my help with the eventual fines. More to *demand* my help.

I said no.

"What?!" he said, shocked and dismayed. It wasn't easy, I hadn't practiced saying no to much of anything and I had made Louie that promise when he was born. To always be there. But I was learning through endless Al-Anon meetings, sometimes two in one day, that being there for an alcoholic actually meant letting go of a lot of things and trusting in a higher power. I was having to learn the "Ed Shipman" way of living by trusting in something bigger to take care of things that were precious to me. I had reached my *worst day* and was hoping that in it were the possibilities for the best one.

Over the next weeks I called Louie occasionally to check on him and at first all he said was, "If you're not calling to tell me you're sending me money, we have nothing to say," before hanging up. I kept going to meetings. Over and over, other members would repeat the basics that alcoholics are born, not created. I couldn't have caused it, I couldn't control it, and I wasn't going to cure it.

When I arrived at Mercy the next month, October, Louie was still in the throes of trying to stay in Huntington, West Virginia, where Marshall is located. He still wasn't listening. I stored away the information about Kelly Home for later, wondering if it might work, and went back to getting to know the people of Mercy.

≈≈

The AfterCare program, another unique program to Mercy because of its size and scope, began with only two people but has expanded to nine team members run by Daniel Nelson, who began as a clinician in Cooke House. AfterCare originally operated on a case-by-case basis, providing care for former residents who came looking for help, the traditional model that many other homes still use. But Father Close noticed the need was becoming more complex and decided to give it all a little structure. Quill Home and Kelly Home were incorporated into the residential program, and the AfterCare program was given a separate and larger budget with new components that were so new when I visited, they were still being designed and created.

"One of the huge things we're implementing now is we're keeping statistics on residents after they've left. The hope is the data will show us what support is working and what is not. We're having brainstorming sessions, asking about what's going right," Daniel said. Education scholarships for former Mercy members, both children and adults, have increased from two to twelve, and the annual budget of ten thousand dollars is now seventy-two thousand. "Our approach in AfterCare is support. We don't call our former residents clients. We call them members. We're not case managers, we're care managers," said Mary Ellen Goodman, who started at Mercy as a youth care worker on the Walgreen campus. "We're walking that path with them. We create a plan with them around their desires, their passions. Most of our alumni don't have intact families or they're dysfunctional. We have a more familial type of relationship than service-oriented."

They're providing the final piece of the circle in residential care that lasts a lifetime. Making sure someone is always there. What is often referred to as 'a net' that ensures we don't hit the streets if disaster creeps into our lives through divorce or illness or something unforeseen.

It is an amazing benefit that is well-funded, enthusiastically supported, and a wonder to behold. While I was visiting, a senior citizen and former Mercy resident called to get help picking out an assisted living facility. Mercy started doing the research on the man's options. Another former resident stopped by to have lunch with one of the members of AfterCare, as he does every week, to feel connected and run a few things by them. They are his touchstone.

For me, it is what hurts most about losing Dad. I have no one to call and spill everything to who will just listen. It wasn't that I expected him to solve anything or that I necessarily had much to say. I just needed to know there was a place in the world where I was always anchored. When I was in Philadelphia at Girard College it suddenly hit me hard that I was alone. I didn't realize how much I depended on that phone call I made every time I was on the road until there was no one to call. The loss was profound.

Throughout my travels I became aware that no one ever loses someone all at once. The person may die suddenly, but the awareness of their absence occurs anew over and over again for a while. It's why I had avoided places my father frequented for awhile. He had a large presence and people were greeting me with, "So sorry about your father," across grocery store lines and in the gym.

The staff in AfterCare realize the possibilities of perpetual loss for members if they become too attached to one staff member so they make a point of having alumni become used to working with several people so that the inevitable turnover is less jolting. If a young man or woman is at Mercy, even if just for one day, they are eligible for After-Care. Mercy has a mission to serve, based on deep convictions, and to practice every day reaching out to as many kids as they can, giving up on no one who wants to change and is actively seeking help.

As it turns out, I got the chance to test that one out.

≈≈

Louie's school, Marshall, sent home a note saying Louie was failing everything and hadn't even shown up for some of the classes. Some of his teachers had never even met him. By now, I was getting better at not reacting and was learning not to draw up a list of wrongs to show Louie. I let it go. I tried to not ask any questions, not offer any solutions, and kept the phone calls brief.

But a bigger question was looming. Getting arrested had sobered Louie up, but he wasn't seeking any other kind of help. He was a dry-drunk; sober but untreated and still on edge and angry. The likelihood of another drink in the very near future was more than a probability. Even he knew the idea of us living together wasn't going to work.

I sent Louie the number for Mercy and Brother Maloney's name, and he called. It was one of the simplest acts of faith either of us has ever committed. Arrangements were made to get him to Chicago for the interview. Bob Danzig, a mentor of mine, a motivational speaker, and a former CEO of the Hearst newspaper chain who had grown up as a foster child paid for the train ticket. He did it without hesitating and wished both of us luck.

Louie was dropped off from college at my home for Thanksgiving break, his things stuffed in the familiar green trash bags, which he deposited in his room before taking off to see his friends. The anger levels were not as high, but we were also better at avoiding each other by this point.

When it came time for him to leave, I put him on the train for Mercy, standing outside in the cold until the train pulled out of the station. I wasn't sure he wouldn't get off. He text messaged me to go home. Twenty-four hours later Louie was in Chicago, standing in front of Brother Brian who Louie towered over at 6'2".

Something began to change here, and I will never be able to explain how it happened. With every inch that I let go, Louie grabbed on to something better. Going from such darkness for so long to a change that was so immediate and all-encompassing was beyond explanation.

Mercy put Louie up for the night in Kelly Home, which had one bed available. He even left me a text message saying, "goodnight mom."

I worked at not growing attached to this new idea just yet. There were still hurdles to get through.

Louie passed all of the tests and evaluations, charming everyone. Brother Brian gave him twenty dollars and dropped Louie off at the train station a few hours early to head back to Richmond on Thanksgiving Day. Louie took off to find a movie theater and ended up running as fast as he could afterward back to the train station, grabbing the train with only minutes to spare. He had another twenty-four-hour trip ahead of him, but instead of snarling he settled in and called me as he passed through different states.

Days later he headed back to Marshall for the last few days of his college career there. I still wondered if it all wouldn't suddenly blow up. His Aunt Diana helped me make the arrangements to rent a small moving truck to get him and his things from Huntington to Chicago. I knew people were wondering why I didn't come with him, why we took such an odd route to say goodbye. But, I knew Louie had to claim this part of his life or it would never work. He had to want to go and actually do something. Close friends understood easily, but others kept asking why I wasn't going. I ignored them.

Inevitably, Louie left behind his old life in his own fashion. He missed the day he was supposed to leave, suddenly stricken with food poisoning from a bad burger. Mercy had to abruptly adjust as a weekend approached and rearranged his arrival and required physical. Brother Brian, who had planned on greeting him, would be off duty. Louie would have to drive in cold.

There was no possibility of waiting till the next week. The dorms at Marshall were closing, and soon he would have no place to stay. He had cut things down to the last possible chance.

Moreover, he waited to get on the road, pushing at the possibilities of failure even then. He started driving at two in the morning with all of his possessions stuffed in what was now tradition—the large green trash bags—which were thrown into the back of the near-empty truck. He had directions but was already exhausted and somewhere in Indiana he started calling me.

It was four a.m., and he wanted to stop driving.

"Where are you?"

"I don't know," he said, tired. "I see a Kroger's."

"Stop there, take a nap in their parking lot. I'll call you back in a couple of hours."

We went on like this all night. Louie called me periodically to check directions and talked to me about what he saw, to keep him company. Already things were changing so much.

At one point he lost his way, missing a turn off, and I guided him across the rest of Indiana by following his progress on Mapquest. Everyone around us was sleeping as Louie talked to me for the first time in a year and a half without the anger I had become so used to. He told me about the small towns he was passing through and what the night sky looked like—the inky blackness with small bright lights and small homes dotting the landscape. It was as if we were together.

It took all night and most of the day before he hit the Chicago area during the evening rush hour. Nate Hope, his new program manager at Kelly Home, took over and guided him in by phone.

I let go of Louie. He sent me a message that night. 'I love you mom,' it read.

Just for that day, everything was perfect. It was more than enough.

The home paid to send Louie back for Christmas. He held the current record for the longest distance away from their residence of any child. I had mixed feelings about seeing him so soon after his arrival there. Everything had been going so well for the two weeks. But Louie still had a court date back in Huntington, and no one else would be around the home Christmas weekend. He got back on the train.

I started to notice something different about myself when he arrived home. I had grown a sense of humor. Louie made a joke with a little bit of an edge to it, and I could laugh it off. I didn't have to respond with what he could have said, should have said. He went outside for a smoke, and I didn't give him a look. It's his life. He went off to find his friends, and I let it go. I didn't call to see where he was or even if he would be turning back up.

And on Christmas Day we sat down to meatloaf shaped like a Christmas tree, as requested by Louie, with mashed potatoes and peas. A Hungry Man meal, a friend of mine pointed out. There were no over-sized presents in the room. There wasn't even a tree or a wreath that year, and it was all okay.

I felt a sense of joy that I had never possessed before, unattached to

Martha and Louie.

anything in particular. I had figured out how to choose to be happy with what is and to feel a sense of gratitude that goes on forever. We were living in the moments instead of the past or the future.

We headed over to my brother's house to say hello. Louie had not seen them since Granddaddy's funeral, and he hung out with the two boys, his cousins. His Uncle Dabney and Aunt Laura greeted him warmly and treated him with respect without asking about school or Chicago. Just for that day, we all enjoyed each other's company. Later I heard him tell one of his friends how much the boys and their little sister had grown and changed.

For the first time in my life, I was looking at my own life—what I had built—and keeping my focus there. It hit me that if I had never agreed to start on this book and instead looked for a safer and more lucrative path, I would not have been witness to so many people willing to change their lives on every level.

Sitting there with Louie, watching football while we ate Christmas meatloaf, I said a thank you for the answer to that prayer I made. I knew that I was loved, forever, by a power greater than myself. And, a thank you for not being at all subtle. Every home I visited was another example of what could be if I could let go, surrender the how or why and do the next right thing that came up.

Finding Mercy Home and a place for Louie was the greatest evidence of it all. Getting to know Louie again and finally finding confidence in myself was part of the new stretch of adventure that had just begun.

An old friend, Maria Butler, who is a beautiful poet, gave me a small, decorated circular box for Christmas that she called a "God box." "Stuff it with everything you want to see happen. Write it down on slips of paper and then let them go. They'll be in the God box." The box is filled to overflowing.

Two months after Louie arrived at Mercy he called me and asked, "What day was it that Granddaddy died?"

"April 21, 2005. Do you miss him?"

"Yeah," he said, his voice catching. "I'd like to see his grave." It was the first mention of his grandfather since the day Louie lowered his ashes into the ground.

Shortly before Louie went back to Chicago, he went for his day in court back in Huntington where all of the charges were dropped and he and another young man were required to pay for the broken window. It was one last thing out of the past that he could let go of. We were doing so much better.

It reminded me of something that happened right after Dad died, before the house was gone. It was a small sign of hope that I held on to during all of those dark months. It began with small green stems that promised to become a swath of late-season wildflowers that were just starting to shoot through the tilled ground. Across the driveway, a carefully arranged zigzag of hollyhocks were showing signs they'd taken root, growing a little bit taller, holding up their broad leaves. I tended to them carefully, willing them to come to fruition. For so long, all they did was grow taller, till they had to be tied to stakes, but no flowers.

The hollyhocks in the garden were my father's, a connection for him back to good memories of his mother and his childhood in the Fan district of Richmond. When he was still with us, but shaky and recovering from an illness, I would sometimes find muddy footprints in the kitchen, and I knew Dad had been standing in the dirt again so he could bend even closer to the small plants and really check out their well-being. I planted both miniaturized acres of hope with my father trying to supervise from a doorway, then the driveway, then right behind me. "Are the hollyhocks too close together?" he asked, a helpful ruler in his hand. "No, it'll be fine," I answered, taking the ruler to make sure and let him see all of the proper care and concern was being taken. "Don't they need to be near the wall?" "No, we can tie them to the green stakes in the shed."

As a group the four of us, my parents, myself, and my son went to a local home improvement store to pick out a good hose that wouldn't twist or kink and a good spray handle that would give us a few choices from mist to hard stream. Dad and Louie pondered over all sorts of gewgaws that were now available for a garden. We made it out with just the two purchases after my mother pointed out, again, that we didn't really need those things and there's no room for anything else in the shed. I watched the three of them, thinking I should want a more glamorous existence than this, knowing I was happy for the moment where I was.

The day after, my father and mother left for the hospital, my father driving, my mother letting him know about any hazards, reading every road sign. It was their system. They were rarely apart and sat through each other's hair and doctor's appointments, waiting for the other one before they headed back home.

Later in the cardiac intensive care unit, my father looked a little shaky and worn out, telling everyone repeatedly how much he loved them. I had wished he'd cut it out, he was far too WASP-y normally. "Okay, Dabney," my mother said, patting his arm in an attempt to get him to stop. He settled back down for a moment, his hands resting on the teal blue prayer shawl covering him before another story and he became animated again. Louie was nervous around all of the tubes and medicine and became testy easily. "Did I scare you?" asked his grand-father. "No," said Louie, but it did.

But, out of the blue, Dad didn't make it and quietly slipped away, leaving an empty space. He died at the age of eighty-one. I suddenly missed being able to help him up and down the front steps to check on the promise of his flowers.

And, just as unexpected, the hollyhock started to bloom early with riotous deep red blooms shooting out everywhere. These stalks that had grown taller but stubbornly refused to even bud suddenly came to life in just a few days. Every flower bed came to life, and for a few weeks the gardens all over the yard accomplished on a grand scale what they had never been able to do before.

Now, I have gone from a household of four to just myself, and I am doing that middle-aged thing of figuring out a life for myself and trying not to call Louie every day to hear about how his new classes at Malcolm X Community College, or what museum he saw that day. I have gone back to the gym and started a new novel, "Sandwich," based on the last two years of my life, and have started having friends over to the little townhouse, all the time.

And, every day, for just a few moments, I say thank you for this day, which is perfect, and for the journey I was given. In the fall of 2007 I am moving to New York City to start my own adventure.

Conclusion

The Possibilities

> "Our deepest fear is not that we are inadequate. Our deepest fear is that we are powerful beyond measure. It is our light, not our darkness, that most frightens us. We ask ourselves, who am I to be brilliant, gorgeous, talented, and fabulous? Actually, who are you not to be? . . . Your playing small doesn't serve the world. There's nothing enlightened about shrinking so that other people won't feel insecure around you. We are all meant to shine, as children do. . . . It's not just in some of us, it's in everyone. And as we let our own light shine, we unconsciously give other people permission to do the same. As we are liberated from our own fear, our presence automatically liberates others."
>
> **Marianne Williamson, *A Return to Love***

The reassurance of knowing where your home is, where you hang your hat, is a basic human need that never leaves us, no matter how old we become. Not a house, but the home we create where familiar objects stay in the spot we last laid them and there are people who love us the best they can figure out that day. For a child a home is the step they forever stand on to reach for the goals in life that can seem scary or at least precarious. It's the information that will seep deep into their bones and guide them, often unknowingly, in their choices of career or spouse. It's a staple and without it, many of us spend way too much time as adults searching for the stability of that missing building block.

If that foundation hasn't been created for a child, all of his focus is trained on finding a place to belong. For the over half a million children in the United States who don't know where home is and can't even say for sure who makes up the elements of their family, finding a haven is essential to their ability to learn and grow. That is where all advocates agree.

But that is where the agreement and the discussion about the well-being of the social orphans of America normally ends. There's a lot of finger pointing and dismissal by the various sides, but no real dialogue that points out the realities of the situation and the possible solutions that are available right now.

If adults can get past the outdated images of nineteenth-century orphanages and accept that foster care is only an element and not the grand solution, there are some very tangible ideas laid out in the stories of these varied homes that will have benefits for not only the children directly involved, but the communities that will accept these children into their folds as contributing adults. Families can find the hope and strength they need, just like Louie and I were so fortunate and blessed to do.

Communities such as San Diego, which decided to work with all of the elements of child care, have already seen a drop in the youth felony rate. Both Washington, DC, and Philadelphia have reaped the benefits of educating at-risk youth, many of whom went on to college and later returned to benefit their neighborhoods.

The Happy Hill Farm Academy has already started reaching out to other states and has begun expanding to accept children from across the country. Most of these successful homes are being courted by overwhelmed cities, such as Baltimore, MD, or Richmond, VA, to teach their methods to these localities.

Internationally, there are some wonderful examples to follow such as Yemin Orde Kedma Youth Village in Negev, Israel, founded in 1953 for young holocaust survivors by Dr. Chaim Peri. It has an average length of stay for kids of six years.

A world away in Israel, a nation so young that it has yet to celebrate a centennial, there is a model for modern-day US orphanages that has been adopted across our country. This new standard not only helps solve the problem of how to raise America's social orphans, but it offers techniques of successful parenting that could be used by overwhelmed parents everywhere.

Called the parent-teaching model, it's a system that uses behavior modification techniques in a smaller setting that more closely resembles the ideal nuclear family. It has already been adopted by many US residential education facilities, like the Virginia Home for Boys and Girls whose story is told in chapter 1. Children are rewarded with points for good behavior, not only toward the teaching parents (always a married couple), but to each other and themselves as well. The expected behaviors, such as following instructions in a timely and courteous manner, earn points, but so does complimenting a fellow resident or offering a handshake and maintaining eye contact with a visitor to the home.

The points translate into privileges that offer the children a chance to safely test their wings within a structured environment. So far, the techniques have proven successful, even with children who were ruled incapable of living in foster care—even though this model closely resembles a type of individual foster care. Boundaries are clearer, as are the rewards, and if there's a particular goal a child is longing for, such as a new drum set, it can be built into the system. All of it is wrapped up into family dinners, bowling nights, homework, and just hanging around the television watching as a group. In other words, it creates a more thoughtful, "normal," family-like environment. The large number of children who are moving on to college or trade schools and into successful adult lives is the best barometer of the method.

The parent-teaching model in Israel was a natural outgrowth of the old kibbutz method of parenting, where an entire village took turns raising the children as a group, which required a lot of listening to each other.

In order, though, for the method to further succeed on our shores, a few obstacles have to be overcome. First, the word "orphanage" in Israel is much more neutral and isn't a lightning rod for stiff opinions, and that makes it easier for advocates of different child care methods to listen, compromise, and pool resources. Say the word "orphanage" in America and you're guaranteed a reaction, and generally not a positive one. The word carries the weight of both real and fictionalized images of work houses, sterile rooms with cots lined up in neat rows, and administrators who were better suited to working in insurance firms than parenting orphans. The truth, both here and in Israel, is closer to the new description of a well-run campus with many child care specialists on hand who genuinely care about every child.

A different trend is the upscale boarding school-style in which children apply to be admitted and have to first meet a minimum set of standards. But, most Americans have never heard of either style. Most don't even know orphanages still exist in this country.

Over time, to combat the bad publicity, orphanages in America changed their names to residential education facilities (REFs) or academies, widened their missions, and moved away from large dorms and cafeteria-style dining halls. Many tore down the large, centralized buildings in favor of the small, quaint cottages that house no more than eight children with room for a married couple—the teaching parents. Children participate in the decision-making of their cottage, from how extracurricular money is spent to what's for dinner.

It's all an attempt to simulate an actual family and give a child a better sense of structure and stability. This may be the answer to foster care advocates who see residential education facilities as cruel or outdated.

The next lesson our country may be able to learn from the Israeli style, which has far fewer government-promulgated rules and is more political in nature. Our prejudice against orphanages in general has led to a glut of regulations that when put into practice are more meddlesome and detrimental. For example, in the cottages they're required to have neon exit signs over every exit that makes everything just a little less like a home. And at one of the homes when a child complained about the choice of after-dinner snacks and called his social worker, the home was required to take him shopping so he could choose his own snacks.

And the entire Israeli system is more centralized rather than our patchwork pattern of state regulations that are often enacted by politicians who've never set foot on the grounds of a residential education facility.

If it is possible for all of us in the United States to let go of our parochialism, we may be able to learn a few new things that could help not only the half a million children who have become the responsibility of the states, but offer something to every household in America—a quantifiable, loving system of raising happy, productive children.

Consider the San Pasquale Academy in Escondido, CA, started by Judge John Milliken in October, 2001, and run by New Alternatives, Inc. There was a reluctance to allow me access to the campus as they strive to be seen as more of an academy than a "home." It's that strange experience again of dividing children into different strata depending on where they happened to land. It's pretending that one group is different from another by virtue of what kind of home they find themselves in. But Judge Milliken is determined to help the children and was willing to meet with me and get the information out to others.

As the number of children in need continues to increase, the number of new foster parents declines. One camp of advocates fights to increase the number of foster parents, and the other fights to give the children who are in need right now the best possible alternative before they age out of the system with nothing at all.

Judge Milliken may have come up with a solution for both and has founded the San Pasqual Academy to prove it. Fortunately, it's working four years after opening, and the judge is taking his idea on the road to places like Richmond and Baltimore. These experiments are the first test cases to see if the idea can be translated to other areas.

But, to understand his approach requires understanding the quagmire of the ties that bind unfit parents to their children and why it's not easy to break them.

The state courts are reluctant to permanently cut the ties among biological family. Rulings have leaned in favor of parents' rights as recognition of the sanctity of the family. The result, though, has been hundreds of thousands of children floating in the limbo of foster care and residential education without a stable home to return to or the legal freedom to be adopted by anyone else.

Efforts have been made to shorten the length of time a child can be held by a parent who's deemed unfit, but the courts haven't reached a strict definition. No one wants to be seen as drawing the boundaries of the American family that are constantly changing. The United States is a blend of a wide variety of cultures.

Meanwhile, advances in communication and travel and the encroachment of TV have helped us settle into a comfortable, bland similarity from sea to shining sea. Thai food can be found in small southern towns, and Texas line dancing is taught in Long Island.

Oddly, the one exception to the rule is at the level of the individual families that make up each suburb or farm or inner city. Each family is as different as a fingerprint. Here is where quirky traditions based on ancestors' cultures and the way Nana Marie did something are preserved and passed down to each new member. The endless variety of family traditions, and how easily we accept this truth, is our most American trait.

We don't have enough of a shared history—very few can trace their lineage back to the American Revolution—but we do possess an accepted set of ideals filtered through our own experiences, our own families, which we argue over endlessly. Preserving the family ties is a constant desire and explains why we'll load up a cranky family sedan with the kids, travel hundreds of miles on overcrowded roads packed with others doing the same thing, just to share a turkey, watch some football, and get back on the road just a few days later thoroughly worn out. It doesn't matter that you know you'll revert to your old pecking order in the family, which you hated; you go anyway. Therefore, it can be difficult for a judge to know when to hang in there or when to call it quits and give a child the opportunity to become part of a new family.

Judge Milliken, the former assistant presiding judge of the superior court in San Diego County, not only recognized this truth, but knew there was an ever-increasing number of children who weren't getting the benefits of a family experience.

"Around 1992, I became very anxious about the quality of service we were delivering to kids.

"Over 2,500 kids passed through the San Diego County courts each year. Mostly, their parents were addicts who didn't bother to return for court dates," said Milliken. "As a result, we didn't have a constant stream of data. We were extending the amount of time people had to reclaim their kids to make sure they were clean and sober.

"The kids were stuck in the foster care system and had stopped bonding from the pain of having bonds broken. Every time a kid formed a bond, we moved them," he said. By the time ties were cut, kids were almost too old to be in the system and were not likely to be adopted and folded into a new, stable family.

No one was coming up with a better plan.

But Judge Milliken, now retired, had an idea that would not only help rebuild as many families as possible, but offer hope and a place to go for those children whose options had run out. In other words, he didn't just recognize a single aspect of the problem and offer one solution; he went after the entire process and ended up changing the dynamics of a community.

He created a comprehensive management system and founded New Alternatives, Inc. Now, every parent that comes into the court system with an addiction problem gets assigned a case manager and placed into treatment within two days. In the past, a parent might have had to wait days or weeks, and the responsibility for finding a bed fell more to the addict.

Drug tests are taken every week, and the results are sent to the court where the cases are reviewed every thirty days rather than the typical six months. By the time the year is up, , the court can tell with impunity who's going to sober up and who is not.

The good news is, more parents realized there was no place to hide and worked harder at becoming clean and sober. The rate of children who could return to their biological family and a safe environment rose dramatically, and the recidivism rate of the parents dropped from a high of 20 percent to 1 percent.

Where it was necessary to cut the parental ties, children were available for adoption and because the cases were adjudicated faster, more were able to find permanent, loving homes. In 1996 there were 290 adoptions and by 2003 there were 700 new families formed—clear evidence of another successful solution.

That left the children who had no home to return to but needed to feel wanted, loved, and be provided with guidance. Then the second half of Judge Milliken's solution was put in place.

All of the children of San Pasqual Academy come from this last group. They are wards of the state with no ties to any family. They come to the academy with some sense of stability knowing no judge will remove them in the middle of the night. But there are a few twists to how the place is run. First of all, its dynamics resemble a fancy boarding school more than a typical residential education facility—even more than Girard College. Children in middle school apply to get in and must meet the main criteria of being self-motivated and able to get along with others, plus be able to complete high school. All of the graduates are expected to go on to college or comparable job training programs. Besides a long list of extracurricular activities and team sports, the academy offers the counseling these children will need and a unique grandparent mentoring program. Senior citizens get to live on campus rent-free in exchange for a contribution of their time one day a week.

Children in the foster care system have noticed the benefits of San Pasqual, and Milliken says it has motivated younger kids to study harder, get the remedial help they may need, and learn to get along in order to be eligible for the school. In 2006 there was a capacity of 135 children, and they are close to that all of the time, but there are plans to build a new dormitory and raise the capacity to 250 by the 2006 school year.

In the meantime, the juvenile felony rate in the county dropped from a high in 1997 of 4,900 to only 2,300 three years later.

Now, Judge Milliken is taking his success stories on the road and teaching the lessons they've learned to other cities and counties that have particularly high rates of juvenile crime and parental addictions. Baltimore, with the help of the Abel Foundation, is close to forming a similar academy, and Washington, DC, is not far behind.

Perhaps Judge Milliken understood something the rest of us have been missing. To heal broken American families will require a holistic approach that encompasses every solution and gives everyone a chance at responsibility with accountability.

There are all sorts of twists to this story. People reach out to children in variations on the theme to fit the locale. The Maya Angelou Public Charter School in Washington, DC, founded in 1997 by David Domenici and James Forman Jr. along with the See Forever Foundation, is located in the heart of northwest Washington. It is a residential educational facility in a unique town, a city burdened with what has so often been called unique problems that the words have become a cliché.

According to reports in the Washington Post, the public school system at one home regularly found dead teachers still on the payroll and still closes buildings because they're unfit. Recently a top union official was found guilty of misappropriating union funds. Meanwhile, the federal government looks over the local lawmakers' shoulders and can step in and mandate under certain circumstances.

Besides the onus of dealing with the district education system and national politicians whose constituent base may be thousands of miles away, the Maya Angelou school (named by the children as a tribute) also has to contend with the typical labyrinth of city and federal regulations that frustrates most residential education facilities, some hostile politicians, and the need for constant fund-raising. That's in addition to nurturing happy, healthy, independent, and educated children—the real reason any of the homes exist.

Despite these difficulties, the Maya Angelou Public Charter School is a success in the heart of the nation's capital. The school is open to students within the DC school system, but, because it's a charter school, it operates under a personalized plan with a separate board of directors. The intent was to form a hybrid that combined the best of public and private schools.

Getting the school off the ground has been a labor of love for the two founders, David Domenici and James Forman Jr., who wanted to offer something more to children living in the shadow of the capital building and in a place sometimes listed as the murder capital of the country. "We were committed to doing whatever it took to help students become successful in the classroom, and we had some talented kids who weren't getting what they needed," said Domenici.

The response from the local community has been enthusiastic and has helped the school to grow and thrive. Besides the founders and staff of the school, Maya Angelou has more 300 weekly volunteers for 230 children at two campuses in the heart of the city. That means, unlike most public schools anywhere else in the country, there are more adults than students, increasing the likelihood of each child successfully completing school. And, at Maya Angelou 70 percent of all students go on to college, a significantly higher rate than any other public school in the district. Several of those children, now in college, were close to dropping out before they entered Maya Angelou, said Domenici.

The school was designed by Domenici and Forman as a holistic answer to juveniles caught up in the court system. The original mission was to teach children the basics, like English literature and geometry, as well as marketable job skills and how to handle responsibility.

They wanted to create a place for children to learn to look to the future and build toward bigger goals, such as a rewarding career. To do that, they knew they needed a place where students felt invested and could see the possibilities. To stay true to that, Domenici and Forman turned over the naming of the school to the children, who chose to honor Dr. Maya Angelou, a poet and educator.

Several years ago, in an effort to offer more, the school expanded by buying three nearby brownstones and boarding twenty-five students who were having trouble keeping up either because of their long commute or due to family issues. The additional space, which includes more extensive supervision of the students, has been a great success, has attracted national attention, and other school systems have requested information on how to duplicate the project.

The See Forever Foundation is hoping to clone itself within DC and is currently raising funds to open two more campuses and add more dormitories, giving more students the opportunity to live in that setting with the option of going home—across town—on weekends and holidays. And, to ensure that the school will be around long after the founders are gone, Domenici and Forman have begun an endowment for a public school to make sure Maya Angelou school can survive any changes in DC politics.

The St. Joseph's Indian School in Chamberlain, South Dakota, founded in 1927 by Priests of the Sacred Heart, is a story of two cultures learning to come together to benefit the Native American children of the plains tribes.

The history of orphanages in general is clouded by misinformation. But, occasionally the bias has been earned and the hurdle is redemption, not among the population at large, but on a much smaller and more personal level, between the institution and the people who were wronged. This is the constant struggle of St. Joseph's Indian School, which was originally created by the Catholic Church to westernize and educate the Native American children of the South Dakota plains. The children were mostly from the Sioux tribe, (Lakota) and the reservation at nearby Ft. Thompson. Students also come from as far away as the Lower Burke, Rosebud, and Pine Ridge reservations.

While no child was ever forcibly sent to St. Joseph's (a practice that did occur at an alarming rate at other Native American homes), the children who lived there had their hair shorn and were forced to leave behind their native language and customs. When forced to reject the way your parents and grandparents live, especially when you come from a culture that revered ancestors and remained close-knit, it pushes the children to disrespect the foundation they started out with in life. Such disrespect of the basic elements that made up who they were and what they must use to build on tore at the individual essence of the child and made success in life more of a struggle, not less. Time passed and people changed, and the institution morphed into a resemblance of the current belief system.

"We serve 100 percent Native American kids," said Michael Tyrell, associate executive director, who, along with his wife, has been at the home for over twenty years. Ninety percent of the children are from reservations, 10 percent are Native Americans with families living in the general population.

However, memories are very long, and anyone who experiences racism knows it can come in very subtle forms as well as written large and when added up is just as stifling. It can be difficult to learn to trust what was once the enemy.

"We have families that want their kids to be here and appreciate the services we provide. But I don't think you see families jumping up and down for St. Joseph's because there are also people on the reservation who don't like us because of the past."

Times have changed at St. Joseph's, and these changes are reflected in every aspect of the curriculum. The home now serves 180 grade school children who live and go to school at the home, and forty high school students who live at the home and go to the public school in nearby Chamberlain. That means that the younger children are the cultural majority, but beginning in high school they become the minority and have their first experiences blending in with the larger national culture of the country.

For the younger children the curriculum is built around their ethnic identity, with Native Americans on staff as both counselors and teachers and includes classes in the fading Lakota language and dialects as well as the use of up-to-date instructional technology. There is an on-campus Lakota museum and classroom that draws 25 to 30,000 visitors every year and annual pow-wows where oral histories are preserved and shared.

Even the Catholic mass has welcomed students in native regalia in an attempt to promote their culture. "Our work here is holistic," said Tyrell. "We can't do the residential [care] without the education, without the support of counseling, without the cultural identity, without the spirituality, and without the recreation."

One large snag in what Tyrell calls the divine mission of raising happy, healthy independent children who are culturally aware is the small number of alumni who successfully go on to, or complete, higher education. The culture shock of going from a close-knit small community devoted to their heritage in a state of only 700,000 people to a fast-paced college atmosphere has proven so far to be too overwhelming for the majority of St. Joseph's alumni.

"It can be things that others might not think of like not having enough pocket money to feed yourself the first couple of days or knowing how to do your own laundry," said Tyrell. Or understanding the cultural difference in shaking hands. On the reservation it's respectful to shake hands gently, almost like holding the other person's hand, but in a job interview an applicant is judged by their firm handshake. Couple this with cultural isolation and the responsibilities of class work and it has often proven to be too much.

This is where St. Joseph's sees its future. They've proposed to South Dakota State University a plan for cooperation, starting from when the children are in the sixth grade to build up confidence levels. Kids in the sixth to eighth grade would visit the campus for a weekend, freshmen and sophomores would be immersed for a week, and juniors and seniors would have the opportunity to take a class for an entire semester.

Right now, they have a student in college in Chicago and are doing everything they can to encourage the girl, just like any extended family, by making regular visits, sending care packages, calling her on the phone, and getting friends in the Chicago area to drop in and offer a helping hand or words of comfort.

The school hopes to expand its mission by becoming a better conduit between high school and college and to create a stronger alumni association (two ideas that aren't mutually exclusive) while continuing to raise children who are citizens of two countries. The children must learn how to successfully bridge two distant cultures without losing touch with who they are.

Setting a good example for the rest of us of what can be accomplished is the new Oprah Winfrey Leadership Academy for Girls at Henley-on-Klip, Meyerton in Guateng Province, South Africa. Founded by Oprah Winfrey and opened in January 2007, the school expects an average length of stay for the girls of ten years.

Success can cause people to go in two different directions. One path is all about hanging on to what has been painstakingly gathered. Fear leads to closed fists and a slight hint of paranoia about everyone else's real intentions. The other path opens up to possibilities, while letting go of any idea of lack or limitation. Oprah Winfrey, whose status as a cultural icon of success was built from the ground up against the odds, has opted for the latter.

In 2000 while visiting Nelson Mandela, Oprah pledged ten million dollars toward a new school and since then added forty million dollars more of her own money. The talk show queen announced she was going to focus her charitable efforts more and chose girls, in particular young South African girls, as her cause celebre. Since then Oprah and her company, Harpo Productions, have sponsored several charitable events such as Christmas in South Africa, but in 2007 the crown jewel of her efforts opened its doors with 152 new students from grades seven and eight. Eventually the school will expand to grades seven through twelve. The new students were drawn from all nine South African provinces to attend the academy and, as Oprah said, she "wanted them to dwell in possibilities."

The new campus has twenty-eight buildings with state-of-the-art classrooms and includes computer and science labs, a library, a theater, a gym, a wellness center, dorms, and a dining hall along with a nearby sports field. "I know that this Academy will change the trajectory of these girls' lives," said Oprah in a press release from the grand opening. "They will excel and pass their excellence on to their families, their nation, and our world." The budget mirrors Girard College in Philadelphia. The A-list decorator made famous by Oprah, Nate Berkus, was in charge of decorating.

Oprah's goal is through education to take young girls and give them a chance at a life full of choices. "This school will provide opportunities to some of our young people they could never imagine, had it not been for Oprah," said Nelson Mandela in the same press release. "The key to any country's future is in educating its youth. Oprah is therefore not only investing in a few young individuals, but in the future of our country. We are indebted to her for her selfless efforts. This is a lady that has, despite her own disadvantaged background, become one of the benefactors of the disadvantaged throughout the world and we should congratulate her for that." To calculate the potential success and understand the framework of what Oprah is stepping into, we can look to Boys Town in Johannesburg and the history of the country's child welfare system.

South Africa is a country that mirrors the United States in several large, key categories. It is a nation conquered by white settlers, the Boers, who imposed a color-based nation that reserved the greatest privileges for whites while denying others rights depending on skin color. Apartheid, or separation, denied through laws and force the most basic of human rights to the native black Africans. It's also a geographically large country with a long history of limited democratic rule, even if so much of its recent history has been intolerable for so many.

Most important to this story, South Africa has had a child welfare system similar to our own—a mixture of foster care and residential education facilities with stories of success and failure on both sides, deeply affected by its own racial inequities, politics, and budget constraints.

When comparing the United States to South Africa, don't assume America has gotten far beyond the question of race. I was told off-the-record that some successful, thriving homes have chosen to close, not because of lack of children or funds—there was plenty of both—but because the population of children at the home had becoming increasingly non-white, and administrators or large donors were unwilling to continue past efforts or support. As recently as the 1990s there were homes still openly barring non-white children from entering their doors, and some had to be sued in order to create change.

From 1990 to 1993 South Africa gradually dismantled apartheid and instituted voting rights. In 1994, voters in the first multi-racial election selected Nelson Mandela as the country's president. This was followed by a smoother transition from segregated to integrated homes than the transition in the United States.

Prior to the end of apartheid mixing black and white within a home would have broken the law and led to the home being shuttered. Immediately after the end of apartheid, homes like the prominent Boys Town welcomed children of other races without an increase in funding from the government and ever since have been working with smaller budgets, longer wait times, and a lot more kids who are eligible for services. Their dedication speaks to the courage and commitment of the school's leadership in doing what is right rather than what would be convenient.

The average wait time for a child entering the welfare system went from six weeks to between two and three months while the amount of funding given to each home by the government has remained relatively static. Much like the United States, the percentage of dollars the government spent on the children it has a large hand in raising is about 12 percent of the amount spent per prisoner. This is a case of focusing on treating the illness rather than preventing the disease—an American way of life.

Additionally, there is an issue that has remained largely an African problem of epidemic proportions—AIDS. Unlike the United States, where AIDS largely affects the adult population in smaller numbers and access to medication is much easier and more acceptable, in South Africa acknowledging you have AIDS is still taboo, and finding the necessary medications, much less their affordability, is often out of the realm of possibility. As a result, mothers give birth to more children infected with the virus, and more children are left without a parental figure. They are orphaned by AIDS.

Into the mix came Oprah with a new residential education facility built on a solid financial foundation with what appears to be a clear understanding of the struggles facing the new endeavor. Some South African child care specialists say the luxury of a leadership academy may turn out to be overwhelming to children who come from dirt floors and one-room huts, thus making their acclimation more difficult, if not impossible. But, the reality is that in South Africa no one yet knows the truth because the idea of giving so much to the native population is new and full of possibilities. At the very least, Oprah is reaching for the most she can offer for what will be a select number of girls.

Imagine what could be accomplished and how far the successful methods could be spread, say to individual families, if we were all more open to the possibility that modern-day homes work, and work well. Imagine if we let go of the idea that any other place to stay is better than a group setting—which, remarkably, is the mind set of a lot of well-meaning social workers these days. Think what might happen if we stopped aping the phrase that orphanages are more expensive, while coyly leaving out the fact that the overwhelming majority of funds are private, costing the public less money.

Imagine if we could wipe the historical slate clean and worked with the children who are here now, aging swiftly out of the system into independence and deserving of everything we can do right now, rather than waiting for an ideal child welfare policy to be developed, agreed upon, and enacted. Imagine if that was our constant paradigm. Imagine the contributions each child would make to the community they grow into, the career they choose, the marriage they make, and the children they eventually raise.

That's where the ideal exists and every time we fail a child by not looking at the obvious; it's the very high price we're all paying for not celebrating and cheering on America's modern-day orphanages.

We must start from where we are—there are not enough qualified foster care parents, and there are more and more children in need—and grasp the possibilities. We have a solution that has already proven it can work, if we, as a country, pay attention.

Appendix A

Parenting Tips

TEN PARENTING TIPS FROM VIRGINIA HOME FOR BOYS AND GIRLS

1. Provide unconditional love and respect.

2. Modeling is one of the most powerful means by which we learn. You are your child's most powerful role model.

3. Praise frequently, criticize sparingly.

4. Maintain high expectations for appropriate behavior and a low tolerance for inappropriate behaviors.

5. Make it your intent to "catch your kids doing something good." Praise them and reinforce the good behaviors, and you'll find you won't have to deal so much with the bad.

6. Teach self-reliance and self-respect by providing opportunities to safely fail or succeed on their own.

7. Listen, listen, listen.

8. Provide structure and consistency for your children. As they mature, teach them to provide it for themselves.

9. Spend time together.

10. Tell them that you love them all the time.

TWENTY PARENTING TIPS FROM GIRARD COLLEGE
(courtesy of the Middle School Residential Faculty)

1. Spend quality educational time with your child.

2. Be consistent, be firm and fair.

3. Learn how to say "No."

4. Spend quality one-on-one time with each of your children every day.

5. Encourage your child to learn to love reading.

6. Remember respect is not given, its earned.

7. Always fully listen to your child.

8. Never let your children forget that you love them.

9. Encourage your child to get involved in school and extracurricular activities.

10. Listen to your child's silence.

11. Acknowledge all who work with your child.

12. Ensure that your children have all the items they need to have a successful week.

13. Good parenting is about relationships, nurturing, and consistency.

14. Pay attention to changes in your child's behavior.

15. Talk to your child and find out what is going on.

16. Be a parent, not a friend; children have many friends but only have one mother and father.

17. Get to know your child's friends.

18. Establish family time: play games, take trips, eat together.

19. Always be encouraging to your child.

20. Know your child, and keep the lines of communication open.

TEN PARENTING TIPS FROM HAPPY HILL FARM ACADEMY

1. Your children must understand clearly what you expect of them.

2. Side-step unpleasant confrontations with your children whenever possible and provide constructive alternatives.

3. Teach your children to think about others and not just themselves.

4. Your children should learn that work is not punishment, but a privilege.

5. Don't be extremely critical of your children.

6. Learn the art of listening to your children.

7. Give your children one of life's most precious gifts . . . your time.

8. Show your children that you really love them.

9. Help your children become responsible, independent adults.

10. Punishment for children should be fair and consistent.

TEN PARENTING TIPS FROM BETHESDA HOME FOR BOYS
(courtesy of Bill McIlrath, Sr.–Mr. Mac)

1. Children learn by example. Life's lessons are more caught than taught.

2. Give children your most valuable resource: time.

3. Admit your mistakes—no one is perfect. Be humble, ask forgiveness.

4. Be a good listener; keep the lines of communication open.

5. Teach children the value of a good work ethic.

6. Provide consistent boundaries; this is where children find security.

7. You either sacrifice when you are young or you sacrifice when you are old. Pay now, play later or play now, pay later.

8. Take your children to church, don't send them.

9. Practice the golden rule: demonstrate, "It's not all about me."

10. Control the TV and the Internet. Know what they are watching.

Bonus: If you are a good parent to your children, you will not have to raise your grandchildren.

TEN PARENTING TIPS FROM MERCY HOME FOR BOYS AND GIRLS

1. Parenting doesn't have to be a struggle. Be firm, fair, and consistent. Avoid power struggles to help build a healthy relationship.

2. Read with your child, maybe not aloud when they're older, but read some of their school assignments so you have ready-made conversation starters at your fingertips.

3. Show your interest in their school work; smile and let them see how proud you are.

4. Attend parent-teacher conferences; listen for the good, and listen for the tips on how to improve.

5. Attach the consequence to the behavior, not to the person.

6. Encourage your children: be positive about what they do well; be patient about what they don't.

7. Remember that boundaries are a healthy part of parenting: be the adult, they'll appreciate it when they eventually become one.

8. Give your children unconditional love, especially when it seems they least deserve it.

9. Have faith that things will work out as they were meant to be.

10. Give them roots and give them wings. You'll be amazed at how far they will soar.

Appendix B

The Shared
Abundance Foundation

*T*he initial mission of the Shared Abundance Foundation, a non-profit organization, is to establish an endowment and college scholarship fund for any individual who grew up in a US orphanage or residential education facility. We know that more kids go on to accredited colleges from this large family than from the general population and we want to continue their efforts to build the American Dream by offering financial support to attend the college or university of their choice. Anyone who has spent a full year in any US orphanage or residential education facility and has been accepted to, or attends, an accredited college or university on a full-time basis is eligible to apply.

The Shared Abundance Foundation has also been established to increase the awareness among the American people of the overwhelming success of residential education facilities. We want to start a discussion of how they can be supported and even further utilized, particularly in today's complicated world, to help raise the more than 600,000 children in this country who are in need of a place to call home.

To get the discussion going, the Shared Abundance Foundation is supporting the research and publication of the book, *A Place to Call Home* by Martha Randolph Carr, and will benefit from a portion of each sale.

The Shared Abundance Foundation has also created The Family Tree Project to help reunite the thousands of alumni of US orphanages who can no longer find each other. To bring these people together we have begun posting old photos, names, and dates on the Shared Abundance web site. Already we have successfully reunited Thomas Campbell, Frank Szemko, and Wayne & Merrill Higgins of the Brookwood Home in Islip, New York.

The Shared Abundance Foundation is also participating in the production of a television documentary, *A Place to Call Home*, based on the upcoming book. The documentary will visit four US residential education facilities with Martha Randolph Carr and give viewers a glimpse into the football games, family dinners, drum lessons, and bowling nights of the children and adults who live, work, and play at America's modern-day orphanages.

If you are interested in learning more about The Shared Abundance Foundation go to www.sharedabundance.us or write to: P.O. Box 29061, Richmond, VA 23242.

To learn more about how to help other alumni of homes reconnect (or if you are an alumnus of a home and would like to begin your own search) go to www.sharedabundance.us and the Family Tree page.

To find a residential education facility in your area contact: CORE: the Coalition for Residential Education, 8403 Colesville Road, Suite 860, Silver Spring, MD 20910. www.residentialeducation.org.

Appendix C

How to Help

The Shared Abundance Foundation
& the Family Tree Project
P.O. Box 29061
Richmond, Virginia 23242

The Virginia Home for Boys & Girls
8716 West Broad Street
Richmond, Virginia 23294

Girard College
2101 College Avenue
Philadelphia, Pennsylvania 19121

Happy Hill Farm Academy
3846 N. Highway 144
Granbury, Texas 76048

Bethesda Home for Boys
9520 Ferguson Avenue
Savannah, Georgia 31499

Mercy Home for Boys and Girls
1140 West Jackson Boulevard
Chicago, Illinois 60607

San Pasqual Academy
New Alternatives, Inc.
17701 San Pasqual Valley Road
Escondido, California 92025

Maya Angelou Public Charter School
See Forever Foundation
1851 9th Street, NW
Washington, DC 20001

The Oprah Winfrey Leadership Academy for Girls
Henley-on-Klip, Meyerton
Guateng Province, South Africa
Send donations in care of:
The Oprah Winfrey Leadership Academy Foundation
P.O. Box 14565
Chicago, Illinois 60693

St. Joseph's Indian School
1 North Main Street
Chamberlain, South Dakota 57325

Yemin Orde
Kedma Youth Village
Negev, Israel

The Imbabazi Orphanage
B.P. 98
Gisenyi, Rwanda

CORE: the Coalition for Residential Education
8403 Colesville Road, Suite 860
Silver Spring, MD 20910

Index